201
Ready-to-Use
Word Games
for the English
Classroom

JACK UMSTATTER

THE CENTER FOR APPLIED
RESEARCH IN EDUCATION
West Nyack, New York 10994

Library of Congress Cataloging-in-Publication Data

Umstatter, Jack.
    201 ready-to-use word games for the English classroom / Jack
Umstatter.
      p.   cm.
    ISBN 0-87628-911-1
    1. English language—Study and teaching (Secondary)   2. Word
games.   3. Activity programs in education.   I. Title.   II. Title:
Two hundred one ready-to-use word games for the English classroom.
LB1631.U47   1994   94-18901
428'.0071'2—dc20   CIP

© 1994 *by* The Center for Applied Research in Education

Printed in the United States of America

10 9 8 7 6 5 4

ISBN 0-87628-911-1

**THE CENTER FOR APPLIED RESEARCH
IN EDUCATION**
West Nyack, NY 10994
A Simon & Schuster Company

On the World Wide Web at http://www.phdirect.com

Prentice-Hall International (UK) Limited, *London*
Prentice-Hall of Australia Pty. Limited, *Sydney*
Prentice-Hall Canada Inc., *Toronto*
Prentice-Hall Hispanoamericana, S.A., *Mexico*
Prentice-Hall of India Private Limited, *New Delhi*
Prentice-Hall of Japan, Inc., *Tokyo*
Simon & Schuster Asia Pte. Ltd., *Singapore*
Editora Prentice-Hall do Brasil, Ltda., *Rio de Janeiro*

Dedication

Thanks to Chris, Kate, Maureen, and our special family and friends.

About the Author

Jack Umstatter, a teacher in the Cold Spring Harbor, New York, public schools, has taught English and literature on both the junior and senior high school levels since 1972 and education and literature at Dowling College in Oakdale, New York, for the past six years.

Mr. Umstatter graduated from Manhattan College with a B.A. in English and completed his M.A. in English at S.U.N.Y.-Stony Brook. He earned his Educational Administration degree at Long Island University.

As a member of Phi Delta Kappa and the National Council of Teachers of English, Mr. Umstatter was recently elected to *Who's Who Among America's Teachers*. He has taught all levels of secondary English classes including the Honors and the Advanced Placement Literature classes. He has led his academic team in capturing the Long Island and New York State championships when competing in the American Scholastic Competition Network National Tournament of Champions in Lake Forest, Illinois.

He is the author of *Hooked on Literature!* also by The Center for Applied Research in Education.

Acknowledgments

Again, I thank my wife, Chris, and my two daughters, Kate and Maureen, for all their help and encouragement.

My friends in the world of publishing, Joe Tessitore, Win Huppuch, and Connie Kallback, have again been terrific throughout this exciting endeavor.

Thanks to Jim Murphy for his French titles.

To all the conscientious English teachers whose efforts to make words come alive… Your students and I appreciate and applaud your skills.

The enthusiasm and encouragement of my students during these past twenty-two years have given me assurance that teachers do make a difference! To you wonderful people, I thank you.

Some of the activities were created with software developed by WISCO Computing in Wisconsin Rapids, Wisconsin.

Definitions used throughout this resource come from *Webster's New World Dictionary of American English, Third College Edition,* Editor in Chief, Victoria Neufeldt, Editor in Chief Emeritus, David B. Guralnik, Prentice Hall, Englewood Cliffs, NJ, copyright 1991 by Simon & Schuster, Inc.

About This Resource

Whether you are just beginning your career as an English teacher or have been in education for a few years (or more), you know that two key components to teaching success are classroom variety and fun. An interesting vocabulary or usage lesson can be both educational and exciting. A dull one can be deadly.

Finding the time to think up creative lessons and still perform your many other duties can be difficult. You want the best for your students, but time does not always allow you to fully utilize your creative instincts. *201 Ready-to-Use Word Games for the English Classroom* was created for you, the concerned English teacher, to help your students increase their word curiosity, expand their vocabulary, and enjoy the wonderful world of words.

The key to every one of the 201 activities is FUN. These classroom-tested activities, which have received very positive student responses, will challenge your kids who will improve their verbal skills and awareness. Whether it is finding palindromes, learning a new proverb, or encountering a crossword puzzle whose answers all begin with the letter "t", your students will look forward to these games. Cryptoquotes, crosswords, mazes, unscramblings, concealed quotations, riddles, and word constructions are just some of the ways these activities will motivate and engage your students in enjoyable learning experiences. Fun and variety. What a great combination!

Section I, "The Roots and Limbs of Our Language," stresses Latin and Greek roots and prefixes, the basis for so much of our language. In addition to numerous activities with roots and prefixes, this section also focuses on the contributions of other languages, namely Italian, Spanish, German, and French.

Section II, "The Tools of Communication," includes words, expressions, clichés, and proverbs used in everyday communication. Several activities involving "doublespeak" language will prove both interesting and challenging to the students.

The thirty-seven activities in the third section, "The World Around You," feature games including U.S. Presidents, foods, animals, musical instruments, and nationalities. Other activities here inform the students about such varied topics as celebrities, sports, math, sciences, cities, and historical figures.

If it's poets, eponyms, writers, or magazines that you want, "The Land of Literature" is where your students belong. Here they will also meet up with banned books, onomatopoeic words, Shakespeare, and the Bible.

"Making Language Work for You" includes twenty-nine activities that make learning grammar and usage painless. Students will improve their knowledge of parts of speech, agreement, sentences, and words often confused—and enjoy the experience!

Section VI, "Taking the Tests by the Horns," prepares your students for the standardized high school and college admission tests that many students must take. S.A.T. exercises and other interesting activities will help your students improve their scores on these important exams.

Section VII, "Just Plain Fun," is exactly that—fun! Here you can select any of thirty-eight creative and fun activities that your kids will certainly enjoy. These games are favorites of my students, and I'm sure your students will feel the same way!

You can choose the activity's implementation. These 201 word games can be used as classwork or homework assignments to introduce or review concepts. Extra credit, research, or group work activities are other suggestions. You can also use an activity as a quick time-filler at the beginning or end of the period. The games make great whole-class activities. Students always enjoy the fun of classroom competition.

Since many of the activities have self-correcting features, such as quotations, hidden words, and famous names, students will see where they have made a mistake and can usually correct the problem. That makes the exercise more fun for the kids and less troublesome for you.

In Poem 1212 Emily Dickinson wrote:

> *A word is dead*
> *When it is said,*
> *Some say.*
>
> *I say it just*
> *Begins to live*
> *That day.*

The importance of words can never be underestimated. Use *201 Ready-to-Use Word Games for the English Classroom* to help teach your students the power and influence of words in their lives. Let them know what they can do with words and what words can do for them. Most importantly, have fun!

Jack Umstatter

Contents

SECTION I
The Roots and Limbs of Our Language ❑ *1*

SECTION II
The Tools of Communication ❑ 29

SECTION III

The World Around You ❏ *61*

SECTION IV
The Land of Literature ❑ *101*

SECTION V
Making Language Work for You ❏ *123*

SECTION VI

Taking the Tests by the Horns ❑ *155*

SECTION VII
Just Plain Fun ❑ *179*

Activity Title	*Skill/Topic*

Activity Title	*Skill/Topic*

Section I

The Roots and Limbs of Our Language

1. ROOTS AND PREFIXES

Match the roots and prefixes in Column A with their meanings in column B. An example word is there to help you. If your answers are correct, you will find three men's names, a fruit, and the initials of the twenty-third U.S. President in the answer column.

COLUMN A

1. ___ fid (fidelity)
2. ___ oper (operate)
3. ___ cogn (cognizant)
4. ___ chron (chronometer)
5. ___ pre (precede)
6. ___ peri (perimeter)
7. ___ aster (asteroid)
8. ___ rect (rectify)
9. ___ para (parallel)
10. ___ per (permeate)
11. ___ fort (fortress)
12. ___ macro (macrocosm)
13. ___ bio (biology)
14. ___ flex (flexible)
15. ___ hum (humus)

COLUMN B

A. workable
B. to correct
C. know
D. life
E. around
F. through
G. large
H. beside
I. strong
J. trust
K. time
L. before
M. earth
N. star
O. bend

The men's names are: _____, _____, and _____. The fruit is a _____. The U.S. President's initials are _____.

2. "ROOT"INELY MATCHING UP THE WORDS

Don't worry about the letters in column B. They are there for a purpose. If you have matched up these root words and their meanings, the answer order will be a quote that is heard by drivers in the Indianapolis 500 on Memorial Day. Good luck!

COLUMN A	**COLUMN B**
1. ___ anima	A. good
2. ___ anthrop	E. to turn
3. ___ bon	E. love
4. ___ brev	G. before
5. ___ cred	I. to follow
6. ___ ego	N. after
7. ___ ex	N. sleep
8. ___ gen	O. former
9. ___ omni	R. short
10. ___ phil	R. all
11. ___ post	S. spirit
12. ___ pre	S. to conquer
13. ___ sequ	T. mankind
14. ___ somn	T. trust
15. ___ vert	U. type
16. ___ vict	Y. self

What are the Indianapolis 500 drivers told to do on Memorial Day? "__ __ __ __ __ __ __ __ __

__ __ __ __ __ __ __!"

3. PREFIX WORD FIND

Twenty-five prefixes are hidden in this word find. Their meanings are listed below the grid. It is your job to find the correct prefixes. The prefixes are placed backwards, forward, diagonally, up and down. After identifying the correct prefixes, write each correct prefix next to its meaning. The first is done for you.

```
T B N R Z G M X L P B G S M B C Q K N J B W X M
H V L B L N J C L Y X V X G M P D G T X B H M P
X P Y K T F L B C P K N B Z C C B K D L W B G H
F T J J J Y H K L D J T T Z M R T R B P C B R Z
X L Q H B R Q Y F K R R L C C X C Q R N M V K Q
P Y C Q B N S P H M G F R H P Q V Q H D G X N Y
W L H W X X X H F I H M Z H S R D Z B Y S M S F
D P S M D X A F L N T T F F N Y G R Z B C V D R
D N O Z V T J N N G C L P G O H A J E F N M D R
W Q P S M L L B T W F F U J E R T N E H Q O V Y
P R O C T A C E D I L L I M A C E D O U D I B C
L P D X T P L B D D H M I B P R V T A N W O J P
P J Y P Y S P T S N V C K X P D N D Z H D G D Q
R Y E V V C W Y B M R Q S B F A R X Y N K Z S G
F H S P G H W N Y O K T S E P T D C B R J B S P
H O W D S P X Q D M S H R F R V K W D P P X J B
P J R S B K F K S J F Y M V F R Z Q H S F F G M
```

Meaning	Prefix	Meaning	Prefix	Meaning	Prefix
after	post	eight	____	half	____
against	____	entire	____	many	____
against	____	for	____	nine	____
against	____	four	____	not	____
bad	____	good	____	seven	____
before	____	good	____	seven	____
before	____	good	____	small	____

Meaning	Prefix
ten	____
thousand	____
twelve	____
two	____

5

4. THE POWER OF PREFIXES

᠕ᡃᡓ᠊ᡄ᠊ᢒᡃ

Knowing prefixes can add greatly to your vocabulary. Match these twenty prefixes with the letter combinations below to create twenty words. Each prefix is used only once. Then unscramble the circled letters to identify the last names of two famous women in U.S. History.

ante	contra	intra	peri
anti	eu	mini	pre
belli	ex	mis	re
bio	hypo	non	sub
con	inter	para	ultra

1. _Ⓞ_Ⓞ dote
2. _Ⓞ_ _ cedent
3. _ _Ⓞ_Ⓞ cose
4. _Ⓞ_ verse
5. _ _ _ marine
6. _ _ _Ⓞ_ _ vene
7. _ _ view
8. _Ⓞ_ _ _ murals
9. _ _Ⓞ_ _ mediate
10. _ _ _Ⓞ dox

11. _ _ _ _ meter
12. _ _Ⓞ_ scule
13. _ _ phonⓎ
14. _ _ _Ⓖivings
15. _ _Ⓞ meditate
16. _ _ _ sense
17. _ _ _ _Ⓞ sound
18. Ⓞ_ _ _ cⒽondriac
19. _ _ _Ⓖraphy
20. _ _ pand

The two famous women in U.S. history are: _ _ _ _ _ _ _ _ and _ _ _ _ _ _ _ _ _ _ _ _.

© 1994 by the Center for Applied Research in Education

5. PICKING AND CHOOSING WORD PARTS

By selecting fifteen prefixes from outside the box and matching them with their fifteen companion parts inside the box, you will construct fifteen words that fit the definitions below. Each prefix and companion part can be used only once. Write your answers on the appropriate lines.

omni   *bene*   *mis*   *poly*

macro

annu

dem

dermic	plexy	agogue
glot	al	adroit
bole	potent	statics
diction	antry	dont
phyte	anthrope	atelist

neo

apo

bio

mal

hyper   *hypo*   *phil*   *ped*

1. _____ all powerful

2. _____ blessing

3. _____ hater of mankind

4. _____ a skilled linguist

5. _____ having large teeth

6. _____ every year

7. _____ beginner

8. _____ loss of consciousness

9. _____ exaggeration

10. _____ study of living organisms

11. _____ a rabble-rouser

12. _____ showy display of learning

13. _____ injection under the skin

14. _____ stamp collector

15. _____ clumsy

6. A HOST OF ROOTS AND PREFIXES

⤙⤚

Match these roots and prefixes with their meanings. The first is already done for you. The words in parentheses in the second column are words from a quote by an American author beginning with "all" . If your answers are correct, the quote reads from #1-20. To make the quote easier to read and also to help in completing the exercise, rewrite the word in ( ) in the blank ( ) after each number.

1. _E_ aud	(All)		A.	before (Twain)
2. ___ ex	( )		B.	carry (from)
3. ___ di	( )		C.	between (comes)
4. ___ ten	( )		D.	away from (by)
5. ___ inter	( )		E.	hear, listen (All)
6. ___ port	( )		F.	see (book)
7. ___ man	( )		G.	hand (one)
8. ___ vis	( )		H.	to, toward (Huckleberry)
9. ___ abs	( )		I.	against (that.)
10. ___ trans	( )		J.	around (comes)
11. ___ ante	( )		K.	conquer (Finn.)
12. ___ cred	( )		L.	forward (writing)
13. ___ ad	( )		M.	one (writing)
14. ___ vinc	( )		N.	two (American)
15. ___ uni	( )		O.	out, from (modern)
16. ___ pro	( )		P.	hold (literature)
17. ___ circum	( )		Q.	heart (Hemingway)
18. ___ dent	( )		R.	tooth (from)
19. ___ anti	( )		S.	across (Mark)
20. ___ cor	( )		T.	believe (called)

Quote: _____ _____ _____ _____ _____ _____ _____ _____ _____ _____

_____ _____ _____ _____. _____ _____ _____ _____ _____. (_____)

7. DIGGING UP THE ROOTS

Your vocabulary will grow with these roots! Twenty-three roots have popped up ready to be buried in this crossword puzzle. Fill in the correct roots and you're on your way to learning and building new words.

ACROSS CLUES

2. to stretch
4. to turn
6. same
7. to carry
8. shape
9. bitter
10. under
12. before
13. to see
15. life
17. to run
18. heart

DOWN CLUES

1. to follow
3. god
5. to write
6. beyond
9. to change
10. to know
11. man
12. to walk; both; around
13. to call
14. to say
16. most important

WORD LIST: ROOTS

ACR	ANTE	CUR	MORPH	SEQU	VERS
ALTER	ANTHRO	DICT	PORT	SUB	VID
AMB	ARCH	EQU	SCI	TENT	VOC
ANIM	CARD	EXTRA	SCRIBE	THEO	

8. BUILDING WORDS

Using one set of letters from each group, construct a word that is defined below. All prefixes, roots, and suffixes will be used.

Prefixes: af, ag, con, di, dif, e, eu, im, in, intra, manu, para, re

Roots: cogn, cumb, dox, fact, fer, firm, gen, gest, greg, gress, numer, pedi, ven

Suffixes: ancy, ate, ation, ative, ed, ent, ical, ics, ion, ize, ment, ous, ure

1. _____ statements seemingly contradictory

2. _____ movement to improve the human species

3. _____ tenure of office

4. _____ a gathering of people

5. _____ to identify

6. _____ to count

7. _____ answering "yes"

8. _____ in the veins

9. _____ not the same

10. _____ to make

11. _____ unprovoked attack

12. _____ thought over and over

13. _____ obstacle

9. IT'S ALL IN THE NUMBERS

৵৵৵

Here is your opportunity to see that things add up correctly. Using your knowledge of number prefixes and words that represent a specific number, as in a decade, fill in the blanks. When you do, a certain pattern emerges. Answer the bonus question correctly, and you'll know if all your answers are the right ones. An example is done for you.

Example: __2__ = mono + mono

1. _____ = mono + tri

2. _____ = di × tetra

3. _____ = nona + hept

4. _____ = score + deca + di

5. _____ = cent – tri (hex + hex)

6 _____ = (pent × score) + (decade × di) + (octa)

7. _____ = kilo – (sept × cent) + (bi × score) + (quad)

8. _____ = (nona + sept) × bi (fortnight + bi)

9. _____ = kilo + score + mono + tri

10. _____ = (bi × kilo) + (quad × deca) + penta + tri

Bonus: What is the pattern of the answers? _____

Here is some space for you to put the prefixes next to their correct numbers:

Number	Prefix	Number	Prefix
1	___	8	___
2	___	9	___
3	___	10	___
4	___	14	___
5	___	20	___
6	___	100	___
7	___	1000	___

10. AVOIDING TWITDOM!

~⌘~

If you're in London and someone refers to you as a twit, don't think you are the recipient of a compliment. The British word twit means a spectacular fool.

Match the correct British term with its American equivalent in the columns below by inserting the correct letter in the space next to the number. Mug up!

a. candy store   f. head   k. scientist
b. car's hood   g. humid   l. small dairy truck
c. druggist   h. line of schoolchildren   m. sporting events
d. easy   i. a little hungry   n. to study something intensely
e. get fired   j. odd   o. substitute teacher

1. ___ He attended the university to become a *boffin*.

2. ___ She uses her *bonce* to figure things out quickly.

3. ___ The *bonnet* flew up when the auto began to move.

4. ___ We visited the *chemist* to receive the proper medication.

5. ___ It was extremely *close* out and we perspired profusely.

6. ___ The teacher led the *crocodile* across the busy street.

7. ___ Since his job was quite *cushy,* he began to gain weight.

8. ___ Have you checked the *fixtures* for the upcoming months so that we can attend as many as possible?

9. ___ Frank tried not to *get the chop* by working harder than ever.

10. ___ The thirsty children had been waiting for the *milk float* to come.

11. ___ If your want to do well on that exam, I suggest you *mug up.*

12. ___ Since I hadn't eaten for half a day, I felt *peckish.*

13. ___ Didn't you find Gerald's behavior rather *rum?*

14. ___ Because he lacked permanent employment, Kevin was a *supply teacher.*

15. ___ For a treat the children were taken to the *sweetshop.*

Name _____ Date _____ Period _____

11. I SAY OLD CHAP!

How well do you understand British words and expressions? Here is your chance to avoid looking like a wally or being called barmy. Match these British words and expressions with their American equivalents. Hidden within the answer column is the five letter British word for infant. Write that word in the space below the last question. Use your bonce!

1. ___ all-in   a. an elevator

2. ___ banger   b. to whine

3. ___ barmy   c. exhausted

4. ___ big dipper   d. tired

5. ___ block   e. lunch

6. ___ brew up   f. an old car

7. ___ fagged-out   g. crazy

8. ___ grizzle   h. apartment house

9. ___ the lift   i. railroad crossings

10. ___ level crossing j. to make tea

11. ___ lumber room   k. to cause to fail

12. ___ prezzy   l. conspicuous fool

13. ___ rise   m. drunk

14. ___ scupper   n. present or gift

15. ___ sticky wicket   o. a salary increase

16. ___ tanked up   p. difficult situation

17. ___ tiffin   q. roller coaster

18. ___ wally   r. a spare room for storage

The British term for infant is _____.

12. SOME GIFTS FROM THE FRENCH

Match these seventeen words associated with foods and beverages. All come from the French language. Bon appetit!

1. ___ VERMOUTH

2. ___ FILLET

3. ___ POTAGE

4. ___ BROCHETTE

5. ___ CROISSANT

6. ___ DEMITASSE

7. ___ FRAPPÉ

8. ___ SAUTÉ

9. ___ CHOWDER

10. ___ VICHYSOISSE

11. ___ APERTIF

12. ___ CROUTON

13. ___ BOUILLION

14. ___ MOUSSE

15. ___ MERINGUE

16. ___ BOUILLABAISE

17. ___ CONSOMMÉ

A. fried quickly in a little fat

B. a clear soup made by boiling meat and vegetables

C. a clear broth, usually of beef

D. small, crisp pieces of toasted bread served in soups or salads

E. soup or broth

F. sweet or dry white wine flavored with herbs

G. smooth, thick soup made with potatoes, leeks and cream, and usually served cold

H. dessert made of partly frozen beverages

I. egg whites mixed with sugar and spread over pies

J. drink taken before a meal to stimulate appetite

K. a rich, flaky bread roll

L. a skewer on which small pieces of meat are fixed

M. small cup of black coffee served after dinner

N. light chilled foods made with egg white combined with fruit or flavoring for dessert

O. a stew of fish, vegetables, and seasonings

P. a thick soup made with clams, vegetables and onions

Q. a boneless, lean piece of meat

13. ARE YOU WISE TO EDELWEISS?

The Sound of Music fans will remember the song, "Edelweiss." An edelweiss is a small, flowering plant. Edelweiss, like the other fifteen words in the first column, are words taken from the German language and used in the English language. Write the correct letter for each of these words in the proper space.

___ 1. KAFFEEKLATSCH	A.	prisoner-of-war camp
___ 2. LAGER	B.	anxiety and depression
___ 3. SAUERBRATEN	C.	abusive criticism
___ 4. EDELWEISS	D.	To your Health!
___ 5. PRETZEL	E.	sudden attack
___ 6. AUTOBAHN	F.	expressway
___ 7. SCHNITZEL	G.	a cutlet, often of veal
___ 8. FLAK	H.	class for young children
___ 9. STALAG	I.	small, flowering plant
___ 10. GESUNDHEIT	J.	musical instrument
___ 11. GLOCKENSPIEL	K.	chopped cabbage fermented in brine
___ 12. KEGLER	L.	informal gathering for coffee and chat
___ 13. KINDERGARTEN	M.	type of beer
___ 14. SAUERKRAUT	N.	bowler
___ 15. ANGST	O.	hard, brittle biscuit
___ 16. BLITZ	P.	beef dish marinated in vinegar with onion

Write a story using *ten* of these words from the Germans.

14. CAN A BAMBINO TAKE A GONDOLA INTO THE BLUE GROTTO?

All the answers to this puzzle are words contributed to the English language by the Italians. Write the correct answers to this puzzle featuring Italian imports.

© 1994 by the Center for Applied Research in Education

ACROSS CLUES

2. disease
5. festivity
6. boat race
10. cave
11. outdoors
12. wild oxen, sometimes domesticated
13. hell
14. complete failure
16. small dagger
17. cone-shaped hill that erupts

DOWN CLUES

1. rain protective device
3. melted rock from a volcano
4. copy of something
5. a minor but well-defined role in a movie
7. a saying
8. boat used in the canals of Venice
9. a baby
10. section of a city made up of a minority group
15. burst of applause

WORD LIST

ALFRESCO	GHETTO	MOTTO
BAMBINO	GONDOLA	REGATTA
BUFFALO	GROTTO	SALVO
CAMEO	INFERNO	STILETTO
CARNIVAL	LAVA	UMBRELLA
DITTO	MALARIA	VOLCANO
FIASCO		

15. ITALIAN FOODS AND DRINKS

We've heard people say, "When in Rome, do as the Romans do." Following such advice, be an Italian for a while and identify these foods and drinks that are Italian favorites.

ACROSS CLUES

2. plant related to cauliflower
3. spiced sausage
7. pasta often baked with cheese
8. long, thin strings of pasta
11. a type of nut
12. pasta in tubes of medium width
13. a beverage

DOWN CLUES

1. cheese
4. thin strips of pasta often served with seafood
5. flour paste or dough used as spaghetti
6. small casings of fresh pasta filled with meat or cheese
7. soup
9. ice cream with heavy cream, cherries and more
10. large shrimp broiled or fried
12. summer squash

WORD LIST

BROCCOLI	MOZZARELLA	SCAMPI
COFFEE	PASTA	SPAGHETTI
LINGUINE	PISTACHIO	TORTONI
MACARONI	RAVIOLI	ZITI
MINESTRONE	SALAMI	ZUCCHINI

16. LATIN WORDS AND PHRASES

The roots of the English language can be found in Latin. Even today Latin is an integral part of the language we use on a daily basis, especially in law and medicine.

Match these twenty latin words or phrases with their English equivalents.

1. ___ ad hoc
2. ___ a priori
3. ___ bona fide
4. ___ ergo
5. ___ homo sapiens
6. ___ id est
7. ___ in loco parentis
8. ___ magna cum laude
9. ___ non sequitur
10. ___ per annum
11. ___ per diem
12. ___ per se
13. ___ quid pro quo
14. ___ requiescat in pace
15 ___ semper fidelis
16. ___ status quo
17. ___ summa cum laude
18. ___ tempus fugit
19. ___ terra firma
20. ___ veritas

a. the present state
b. rest in peace
c. with great praise
d. the human species
e. in place of the parent
f. for a special purpose
g. daily
h. from cause to effect
i. always faithful
j. truth
k. therefore
l. something not following logically
m. in good faith
n. annually
o. something for something
p. that is
q. for itself
r. time flies
s. with highest praise
t. solid ground

17. OWSDR MORF HET PSHSINA

The letters of the words in this exercise's title, WORDS FROM THE SPANISH, have been scrambled up. The same goes for each of the sixteen words in this activity. Another trait these sixteen words share is that they are all Spanish gifts to the English language. Write the letters in the spaces provided.

1. ORCOCHCKA

1. _ _ _ _ _ _ _ _

2. OOTTMA

2. _ _ _ _ _ _

3. NTAU

3. _ _ _ _

4. ACABDRARU

4. _ _ _ _ _ _ _ _

5. OOQTISUM

5. _ _ _ _ _ _ _ _

6. ANOEC

6. _ _ _ _ _

7. DRNTOOA

7. _ _ _ _ _ _ _

8. RGICA

8. _ _ _ _ _

9. OPOTAT

9. _ _ _ _ _ _

10. ACHOUG

10. _ _ _ _ _ _

11. ACAOC

11. _ _ _ _ _

12. JAIRANUAM

12. _ _ _ _ _ _ _ _ _

13. ABANNA

13. _ _ _ _ _ _

14. TNOCOCU

14. _ _ _ _ _ _ _

15. CHPNOO

15. _ _ _ _ _ _

16. EREQBUAB

16. _ _ _ _ _ _ _ _

18. TELL ME WHERE YOU'RE FROM!

Seventeen words derived from languages all over the globe are gathered here in this matching column. With the help of your dictionary, identify each word's derivation by writing the correct letter in the space.

___ 1. LASSO	A. Yiddish	
___ 2. SOVIET	B. African	
___ 3. SAFARI	C. Italian	
___ 4. PEDAGOGUE	D. Russian	
___ 5. GESTAPO	E. Latin	
___ 6. WOK	F. Hebrew	
___ 7. KOSHER	G. French	
___ 8. FEZ	H. Australian	
___ 9. GURU	I. Scottish	
___ 10. BOOMERANG	J. Chinese	
___ 11. ASSASSIN	K. Turkish	
___ 12. CLAN	L. Indian	
___ 13. KNISH	M. Greek	
___ 14. KARATE	N. Arabian	
___ 15. POTPOURRI	O. Japanese	
___ 16. ARIA	P. German	
___ 17. TOGA	Q. Spanish	

After you and your classmates have found the meanings of these words, write a news story including at least ten of these words.

19. DO AS THE ROMANS DO

Roman numerals are found in the twenty words below. Match the words with the total of Roman numerals found within the word. As an example, radii is 502 since d plus i plus i equals 502. Count each letter separately so that XL as found in AXLE equals 60, not 40. Write your answers in the appropriate spaces.

1. ___ EXIT	A.	61
2. ___ IDYLLIC	B.	1151
3. ___ CODIFY	C.	252
4. ___ MULTITUDINOUS	D.	1001
5. ___ CLIMB	E.	1503
6. ___ DIMINISH	F.	1052
7. ___ LICORICE	G.	2000
8. ___ VEXATION	H.	2501
9. ___ CAVIL	I.	601
10. ___ DRIED	J.	11
11. ___ MADDER	K.	702
12. ___ DOCILE	L.	203
13. ___ SIMILE	M.	1500
14. ___ AXIOM	N.	651
15. ___ MEMORIZED	O.	1552
16. ___ DEVIL	P.	16
17. ___ ILLICIT	Q.	107
18. ___ DADDY	R.	1011
19. ___ INVOICE	S.	156
20. ___ EXILE	T.	556

Name five U.S. States that have Roman numerals in them. What is the total of each state?

20. CRAZY EIGHTS

Eight words, each having eight letters, have been divided up within the four columns below. Using two letters from each consecutive column, find the eight words hidden within the columns. Write your answers in the spaces below the columns. The first word is already found for you.

A	B	C	D
C̶O̶	CO	AT	A̶L̶
DE	LL	EN	ED
ED	MA	ND	ER
EX	M̶M̶	NT	IC
HA	ND	RA	LY
PO	SI	SO	ME
RO	TE	TI	TE
SU	UC	U̶N̶	VE

The eight words found in these columns are:

<u>communal</u>   _____

_____   _____

_____   _____

_____   _____

21. GRAB BAG

Forty words are in this grab bag of compound words. Match the words that go together and you become the winner! The first one, bracelet, is done for you. The other nineteen pairs are up to you. Write your answers in the spaces provided.

able	*car*	*grim*	*kerchief*	*neck*	*through*
ace	*cut*	*hand*	*knee*	*part*	*up*
age	*depend*	*hard*	*lace*	*patron*	*way*
art	*doctor*	*he*	*leaf*	*ridge*	
ate	*feat*	*her*	*lip*	*stick*	
bye	*gin*	*ice*	*loose*	*street*	
cap	*good*	*just*	*mar*	*tack*	

1. <u>bracelet</u>

2. _____

3. _____

4. _____

5. _____

6. _____

7. _____

8. _____

9. _____

10. _____

11. _____

12. _____

13. _____

14. _____

15. _____

16. _____

17. _____

18. _____

19. _____

20. _____

Bonus: There are several U.S. states that are compound words, several that are three words in a row, and at least two that have four words in them. How many of these can you name without using proper nouns found in the state's name?

22. NOUNS SHARING THE SAME ADJECTIVE

What do pack, shoulder, and turkey have in common? They all share the adjective *cold!* Cold pack, cold shoulder, and cold turkey are all expressions containing the word *cold*. On the line next to each group, write the adjective that is common to the words in that group.

1. _____ dock, rot, run

2. _____ calf, parachute, rule

3. _____ handed, triangle, wing

4. _____ band, shot, wheel

5. _____ fisted, mouthed, quarters

6. _____ headed, opera, verse

7. _____ blanket, nurse, suit

8. _____ cause, generation, hope

9. _____ alert, carpet, herring

10. _____ break, news, vibes

11. _____ cap, collar, flag

12. _____ box, cream, pop

13. _____ age, hat, school

14. _____ nothings, potato, tooth

15. _____ bridge, buttress, saucer

16. _____ Ages, Continent, horse

17. _____ box, carrier, opener

18. _____ bell, lining, screen

19. _____ beret, card, thumb

23. ODDS AND EVENS

Here's your chance to create words in a methodical way. Follow the directions for creating words.

(Odd Row)   **A C E G I K M O Q S U W Y**

(Even Row)   **B D F H J L N P R T V X Z**

A. *Directions:* Using only letters from the odd row, create five words having five or more letters. *Quick* is a word that fits this pattern. A letter may be used twice in a row and /or more than once. Write your answers here:

_____ _____ _____ _____ _____

B. *Directions:* Starting with a letter from the even row and then alternating rows, create five words having five or more letters in them. *Decline* is a word that fits this pattern. A letter may be used twice in a row and/or more than once. Write your answers here.

_____ _____ _____ _____ _____

C. *Directions:* Starting with a letter from the odd row and then alternating rows, create five words having five or more letters in them. *Store* is a word that fits this pattern. A letter may be used twice in a row and /or more than once. Write your answers here.

_____ _____ _____ _____ _____

24. A SCORE OF WORDS

❦

Exercise your brain cells by finding words within a longer word. Find twenty words in each of the following longer words. Each of your answers must consist of at least four letters. Plurals are not accepted. Write your answers on the lines below the words.

WONDERFUL

1. _____	6. _____	11. _____	16. _____
2. _____	7. _____	12. _____	17. _____
3. _____	8. _____	13. _____	18. _____
4. _____	9. _____	14. _____	19. _____
5. _____	10. _____	15. _____	20. _____

SWITZERLAND

1. _____	6. _____	11. _____	16. _____
2. _____	7. _____	12. _____	17. _____
3. _____	8. _____	13. _____	18. _____
4. _____	9. _____	14. _____	19. _____
5. _____	10. _____	15. _____	20. _____

SANDERS

1. _____	6. _____	11. _____	16. _____
2. _____	7. _____	12. _____	17. _____
3. _____	8. _____	13. _____	18. _____
4. _____	9. _____	14. _____	19. _____
5. _____	10. _____	15. _____	20. _____

25. HOW A GREENHOUSE BECAME A TINSMITH

⚜

Here's a way to have fun by building words to become other words. Start with a compound word made up of any two words. Using the second word of that compound word, add a new word to make that combination a new compound word. Thus "makeshift" can become "shiftless" and "shiftless" can become "lesson".

Here is an example of a twenty-step word construction:

greenhouse	*houseboat*	*boatman*	*manhandle*	*handlebar*	*bartender*
tenderloin	*loincloth*	*clothbound*	*boundless*	*lesson*	*onion*
ionone	*onetime*	*timeout*	*outpost*	*postwar*	*warden*
dentin	*tinsmith*				

Construct your own word buildings in the spaces below.

STARTING WORD   **STARTING WORD**   **STARTING WORD**

_____ _____ _____

_____ _____ _____

_____ _____ _____

_____ _____ _____

_____ _____ _____

_____ _____ _____

_____ _____ _____

_____ _____ _____

_____ _____ _____

_____ _____ _____

_____ _____ _____

26. WE NEED AL!

∽ɕ~ℐ∾

AL is not a person. It is a two letter combination added to the words pet, flow, and tent to make the words petal, fallow, and talent. Find other two letter combinations that can be used to make the words in each group into three new words.

TWO LETTERS	OLD WORDS	NEW WORDS
1. _____	cad, port, bad	_____
2. _____	read, cater, an	_____
3. _____	bill, pal, mall	_____
4. _____	rely, lid, other	_____
5. _____	card, lest, click	_____
6. _____	come, lo, at	_____
7. _____	be, them, mage	_____
8. _____	son, man, ken	_____
9. _____	tater, cap, art	_____
10. _____	pal, feral, real	_____
11. _____	row, tee, hear	_____
12. _____	one, ink, ash	_____
13. _____	flow, bow, dude	_____

Construct four more sets of words like the ones above.

Section II

The Tools
of Communication

27. MATCH THEM WITH THEIR MATES

Here are twenty "masculine" names. Write their female equivalents on the line next to the number.

1. _____ abbot

2. _____ aviator

3. _____ baronet

4. _____ billy goat

5. _____ boar

6. _____ bull

7. _____ colt

8. _____ duke

9. _____ earl

10. _____ emperor

11. _____ hero

12. _____ king

13. _____ lad

14. _____ lord

15. _____ patriarch

16. _____ ram

17. _____ rooster

18. _____ tiger

19. _____ tsar

20. _____ usher

28. "... LEND ME YOUR EARS"

❧

This famous line from William Shakespeare's play, *JULIUS CAESAR,* is missing an important part. If you know that the missing portion includes the threesome, "Friends, Romans and Countrymen," you are off to a good start in this activity. On the blank line after the words in column A, write the letters of the words that make up the other two parts of the threesome from columns B and C. The first one is already done for you.

COLUMN A		COLUMN B		COLUMN C	
1. beg	B, Q	A	book	A	barrel
2. bell	_____	B	borrow	B	be merry
3. do	_____	C	chocolate	C	candle
4. eat	_____	D	Dick	D	charity
5. earth	_____	E	drink	E	fire
6. faith	_____	F	equality	F	fraternity
7. gold	_____	G	frankincense	G	future
8. hook	_____	H	hope	H	go
9. liberty	_____	I	line	I	Harry
10. lion	_____	J	look	J	listen
11. lock	_____	K	place	K	mi
12. past	_____	L	present	L	myrrh
13. readin'	_____	M	re	M	'rithmetic
14. ready	_____	N	ritin'	N	show
15. stop	_____	O	set	O	sinker
16. Tom	_____	P	stock	P	song
17. vanilla	_____	Q	vidi	Q	steal
18. veni	_____	R	wind	R	strawberry
19. win	_____	S	witch	S	vici
20. wine	_____	T	women	T	wardrobe

© 1994 by the Center for Applied Research in Education

29. BREAK A LEG!

Body parts are often found in words and expressions. "Break a leg" means good luck to a per-former. In each of the defined expressions below, fill in the missing body part. Words may be used more than once. The first is done for you.

1. travel at break <u>neck</u> speed: to go very fast

2. an _____ and a _____: a very great amount of money

3. _____ service: insincere expression of respect or support

4. right-_____ man: the most reliable supporter

5. keep a stiff upper _____: to stand brave and firm

6. _____-jerk reaction: automatic and predictable response

7. keep an _____ to the ground: to listen carefully; be wary

8. _____s up: to be alert

9. monkey off my _____: to be rid of a major problem

10. flat _____: slang for a policeman

11. ice in the _____s: cannot be frightened; cool in a tense situation

12. _____him up: support

13. _____ gay: a bunch of flowers

14. _____ broken: overwhelmed with sorrow

15. _____ hold: means of surmounting problems

16. _____ the line: to follow orders

17. _____-catcher: one who attracts attention

18. _____ session: a class session where a team studies and discusses plays

19. _____ nail sketch: small or concise

20. _____ to _____: agreement

21. Achilles' _____: a weakness

Can you think of more words or expressions that have body parts in them?

© 1994 by the Center for Applied Research in Education

30. THE COLORFUL WORLD OF WORDS

Have you ever felt blue? Why are people green with envy? Stop for a minute and think of how often we use colors to describe people, places, things and ideas in general. Fill in the missing colors in these expressions that use colors to get their point across. Each expression is followed by its meaning in parenthesis.

1. once in a _____ moon (not often)
2. _____ tape (rules and regulations that tend to frustrate)
3. _____ jackets (wasps or hornets)
4. _____ magic (sorcery)
5. _____ lightning (homemade whiskey)
6. every cloud has a _____ lining (basis for hope)
7. to _____ bag it (carry your lunch to school, work, etc.)
8. _____ card (registration card giving permission to reside and be employed in the United States
9. _____ and _____ (bruised)
10. to see _____ (angered)
11. in the _____ (in debt)
12. in the _____ (solvent)
13. _____ alert (warning of danger)
14. _____ matter (brains)
15. _____ book (student examination book)
16. _____ belly (coward)
17. _____ belt (karate's highest award)
18. _____ carpet (impressive welcome)
19. _____ cap (a wave)
20. _____ -chip (high priced stock with good returns)
21. _____ room (entertainer's waiting room)
22 _____ beard (an old man)
23. out of the _____ (unexpected)
24. _____ law (law prohibiting Sunday activities)
25. _____ ball (to ostracize)

Can you and your classmates think of more terms or expressions using colors? Try it!

© 1994 by the Center for Applied Research in Education

31. IS THIS YOUR ACHILLES' HEEL?

During the famous Trojan War, Achilles, the brave Greek leader and soldier, was fatally wounded when Paris struck him with an arrow in his heel, the sole vulnerable spot on Achilles' body. Though not under the most auspicious circumstances, the cliché, *Achilles' heel,* was born to mean one's vulnerable or susceptible spot.

Fill in the missing blanks of these defined clichés. Then using the circled letters, identify the woman whose beauty was the cause of the Trojan War.

1. Achilles' _ _ _ _: vulnerable or susceptible spot

2. hit _ _ _ _ _ the belt: unfair behavior

3. _ Ⓞ _ _ _ of heart: to revise your opinion or feeling about a person or issue

4. _ _ _ _ as a doornail: not responsive

5. _ _ _ Ⓞ _ room: sufficient space

6. Ⓞ _ _ _ _ wheel: person or thing that is more than needed

7. it's _ Ⓞ _ _ to me: not understandable

8. _ _ _ _ and dry: stranded

9. ignorance is _ _ _ _ _: at times it's better not to know

10. _ _ _ _ the gun: to act prematurely

11. kit and _ _ _ _ Ⓞ _ _ _: everything

12. lay it on the _ _ _ Ⓞ: to speak frankly

13. _ _ _ or never: the final opportunity to act on an item

14. on the _ _ _ _ _: not drinking alcoholic beverages

15. the _ _ Ⓞ is mightier than the sword: words can inflict more pain than physical actions

16. quiet as a _ _ _ _ _: not heard

17. _ Ⓞ _ _ _ _ is sweet: getting back at someone is satisfying

18. talk Ⓞ _ _ _ _ Ⓞ: to discuss the central issue or point

19. _ _ _ _ _ _ into thin air: to disappear completely

20. wheel and _ _ _ Ⓞ: to behave aggressively for one's own gain

The woman whose beauty was the cause of the Trojan War was __ __ __ __ __ __ __ __ __ __.

32. PALINDROMES

Palindromes are words that read the same frontward or backward. Mom and dad are common examples of palindromes. Fill in the palindromic answers to the following clues and then unscramble the letters found in the circles to compose a palindromic phrase that tells what kind of political entertainment pleased the crowd.

1. _ _ O _ O radio detecting device

2. _ O _ _ _ even

3. O _ _ _ O title for a lady

4. _ _ _ _ to peek

5. _ _ _ to move with a slight jerk

6. O _ O _ an act of heroism

7. O _ _ _ to blow a horn

8. _ _ O _ 12 pm

9. O _ _ _ a slang term for a dumb person

10. _ _ O _ a ship's deck

11. _ _ _ _ _ a rotating mechanical part

12. _ _ _ _ _ _ more embarrassed

13. _ _ _ _ _ one person performances

14. O _ _ _ _ to allude to

15. O _ _ _ O relating to a city and citizenship

16. O _ _ _ _ numbers on a chart

17. _ _ _ _ O principle or doctrine

18. _ _ O _ O Iranian rulers

19. _ _ _ O _ long stories

20. _ _ O _ _ an Eskimo canoe

21. _ O _ a hurricane's center

PHRASE: _ _ _ _ _ _ _ _ _ _ _ _ _ _ _ _ _ _ _ _ _ _ .

33. UNSCRAMBLING PROVERBS

Unscramble these eleven proverbs. Then discuss their meanings with your classmates.

1. good die the only young.

   _____

2. be boys will boys.

   _____

3. over milk don't spilled cry.

   _____

4. leap look you before.

   _____

5. is believing seeing.

   _____

6. still deep waters run.

   _____

7. horse look in mouth don't a gift the.

   _____

8. the wheel the oil squeaky gets.

   _____

9. survive strong the only.

   _____

10. is as strong weakest link a its chain as.

    _____

11. makes fonder the grow absence heart.

    _____

34. PROVERBS

A proverb is a saying that offers a piece of advice. From the list below fill in the missing word from each of these proverbs. Then discuss each proverb's meaning in class.

actions	*cleanliness*	*fool*	*name*	*safe*	*twice*
angels	*company*	*hesitates*	*pot*	*stones*	*wins*
best	*divided*	*hurt*	*rope*	*sufficient*	*woman's*

1. A watched _____ never boils.

2. He who _____ is lost.

3. Slow and steady _____ the race.

4. Misery loves _____.

5. _____ speak louder than words.

6. Fools rush in where _____ fear to tread.

7. Fool me once, shame on you; fool me _____, shame on me.

8. A _____ and his money are soon parted.

9. He who laughs last, laughs _____ .

10. You always _____ the one you love.

11. A house _____ against itself cannot stand.

12. People in glass houses should not throw _____.

13. _____ is next to godliness.

14. It's better to be _____ than sorry.

15. A rose by any other _____ would smell as sweet.

16. Give a man enough _____ and he'll hang himself.

17. A word to the wise is _____.

18. A _____ work is never done.

© 1994 by the Center for Applied Research in Education

35. DOUBLESPEAK

In his entertaining and educational book, *Doublespeak,* William Lutz gives many real-life examples of how language is used to deliberately confuse or distort the facts of the matter. Did you know that a tax increase is a "revenue enhancement"? An invasion is a "pre-dawn vertical insertion." These are just a few of the many doublespeak examples cited by Mr. Lutz.

Here are twenty more doublespeak items. Match the two columns to see how language can play tricks on all of us!

1. ___ hammer

2. ___ reactor's explosion

3. ___ toilet stall

4. ___ desks

5. ___ house burns down

6. ___ smelling something

7. ___ acid rain

8. ___ cemetery plot

9. ___ bus driver

10. ___ robbery

11. ___ gas station attendant

12. ___ fire alarm bell

13. ___ job layoff

14. ___ massacre

15. ___ tent

16. ___ toothpick

17. ___ pencil

18. ___ bomb

19. ___ air crash

20. ___ war

a. underground condominium

b. involuntary conversion of property

c. movable partitions–privacy

d. rapid fuel relocation

e. vertically deployed anti-personnel device

f. frame-supported tension structure

g. certified adolescent transportation specialist

h. poorly buffered precipitation

i. organoleptic analysis

j. premature impact with ground

k. lethal intervention

l. mad confusion

m. downsizing personnel

n. authorized transaction

o. pupil stations

p. petroleum transfer engineer

q. portable, hand-held communications inscriber

r. manually-powered, fastener-driving impact device

s. combustion enunciation

t. interlocking slide fastener

Devise your own doublespeak for these three terms: (a) unit test   (b) root canal   (c) high school graduation.

36. MORE DOUBLESPEAK

❧

Here are fifteen more words and expressions from *Doublespeak* by William Lutz. Write the appropriate word next to its *Doublespeak* definition.

blackmail payments
chicken coop
flashlight
girdle
killing
lies
military retreat

neutron bomb
nuclear reactor fire
nuclear warhead
plutonium contamination
remedial courses
truck's mud flaps
war
wellness

1. _____ a breach of containment

2. _____ laundered money

3. _____ splash and spray suppression devices

4. _____ physics package

5. _____ emergency exit light

6. _____ rapid oxidation

7. _____ inoperative statements

8. _____ radiation enhancement device

9. _____ unlawful or arbitrary deprivation of life

10. _____ optimum physical and mental potential

11. _____ college preparatory adult education

12. _____ paramilitary operation

13. _____ form persuader

14. _____ single-purpose agricultural structure

15. _____ straightening of the front

As a fun exercise, write a short news report using doublespeak words and expressions concerning a happening in your town or school.

37. AS EASY AS PIE!

"As easy as pie" is a cliché, an overused expression. The word *cliché* is derived from the French word *clicher* meaning to stereotype. Though clichés are overused, they are used to communicate an idea.

Choose a word from the list below to complete clichés 1–20. Write the correct word on the blank line. The first one is done for you.

April	*dozen*	*if's*	*old*	*toe*
behind	*fiddle*	*light*	*quick*	*under*
cold	*highway*	*mad*	*rain*	*x*

1. _____rain_____ or shine: regardless of what happens

2. fit as a _____: in very good condition

3. a dime a_____: very plentiful and available

4. _____ marks the spot: designating the location

5. _____ as feather: having little weight

6. _____ the eight ball: to be in a dangerous or unpleasant position

7. _____ as the hills: having great age

8. _____ robbery: very expensive

9. _____ as a wink: very swiftly

10. _____, and's, and but's: excuses

11. _____ the line: to do exactly as requested

12. _____ showers bring May flowers: good comes from bad

13. _____ as a hatter: crazy

14. _____ the weather: ill

15. _____ turkey: to stop a bad habit immediately and completely

38. HAVE YOU MET MY BETTER HALF?

One's better half is a cliché for one's spouse. The other nineteen clichés in this matching column will test your knowledge of more difficult clichés. When you have correctly matched these two columns, find a cliché in the answer column and write it below the matching column.

1. ___ my better half   a. public uproar

2. ___ bête noire   b. satisfactory

3. ___ catch as catch can   c. one like oneself

4. ___ egg on one's face   d. not to be dismissed easily

5. ___ foam at the mouth   e. spouse

6. ___ go scot-free   f. to court danger

7. ___ hue and cry   g. by any method

8. ___ kindred spirit   h. obstacle

9. ___ lie low   i. put aside funds for the future

10. ___ name of the game   j. exactly

11. ___ not to be sneezed at   k. to behave formally

12. ___ play with fire   l. true purpose

13. ___ salt away   m. nuisance

14. ___ square deal   n. to embarrass oneself

15. ___ stumbling block   o. conceal one's intentions

16. ___ to a T   p. avoid giving a definite answer

17. ___ up to snuff   q. to act uncontrollably

18. ___ hem and haw   r. to let off without punishment

19. ___ pull the wool over one's eyes   s. honest arrangement

20. ___ stand on ceremony   t. to deceive

The hidden cliché is _____.

39. CLEO, QUEEN OF THE CLICHÉS

Cleo has written a letter to her best friend. As usual, she has included many clichés, twenty to be exact. Underline the clichés and be ready to explain their meanings. Line numbers are included for easy reference.

Dearest Maude,

1   Hello! It is as cold as ice here. The land, which is
2   normally flat as a pancake, now has a blanket of snow that is
3   as smooth as glass. The distant mountains are silhouetted
4   against the sky. Rather than hearing the patter of rain or its
5   raining cats and dogs, I hear only the ocean's roar. The whole
6   scene is as pretty as a picture. This is God's country!

7   At the crack of dawn, it is as black as coal here. Ominous
8   silence pervades. What looms on the horizon is beautiful. The
9   morning's mist is as fresh as a daisy. Trees stand like sentinels
10   guarding the morn. Little by little in all its glory nature
11   is magnificently showing her beauty. With all as white
12   as snow, I am exhilarated! I certainly have the life of Riley!

Yours truly,

Cleo

40. THE *NEWS* REPORTS:
HANK SMITH LEADS A DOG'S LIFE!

If you don't know clichés and their meanings, you might be confused by this headline about Mr. Hank Smith. A dog's life means that one has a miserable existence. Using the words in the list below, fill in the headlines' missing words. All of these headlines feature the names of animals or foods. When all the words are filled in, discuss what these clichés mean with your classmates.

apple	clam	fox	pancake
beaver	dog	horse	peas
bird	duck	lion	pie
cheese	egg	nuts	skunk

1. "Geraldine Jones is the dark _____ in this election."

2. "Doctor Weaver states, 'An _____ a day keeps me away.'"

3. "Coach tells team it's time to beard the _____."

4. "Lottery winner is now as happy as a _____."

5. "Youngsters complain that Mike thinks he's so special, the big _____."

6. "Hit by the powerful fullback, Frank felt he was as flat as a _____ ."

7. "Folks enjoy a complete meal from soup to _____."

8. "Intoxicated man found to be drunk as a _____."

9. "Kindred spirits are like two _____ in a pod."

10. "Candidate is busy as a _____ seeking votes."

11. "Student feels free as a _____ now that exams are over."

12. "Criminal described by judge as a 'bad _____.'"

13. "Nosy boss feels the need to have a finger in every _____."

14. "Colleagues say that Sharon was dumb like a _____."

15. "Vagrant leads a _____'s life."

16. "Criminals talk about the sitting _____ they want to murder."

Name _____ **Date** _____ **Period** _____

41. HOW AM I SUPPOSED TO TAKE THAT?

Words can have different meanings depending upon their intended use. For each of these twenty questions, identify the word that fits the definitions next to it. As a bonus, identify the two three-letter words that have more meanings than almost any other words in the English language. These two bonus answers begin with letters that follow one another in the alphabet.

WORD	DEFINITIONS
1. _ _ _	(1) a human being (2) to fortify
2. _ _ _ _ _	(1) stigmatize (2) a mark denoting the product's maker
3. _ _ _	(1) a cattle call (2) not high or tall
4. _ _ _ _ _	(1) a sprite (2) a maxim
5. _ _ _ _ _	(1) small rodent (2) small hand-held computer device
6. _ _ _ _ _ _	(1) to divide (2) to cling
7. _ _ _ _ _	(1) to woo (2) where justice is administered
8. _ _ _ _	(1) an equal (2) to look intently
9. _ _ _ _	(1) waist sash (2) to smash
10. _ _ _ _	(1) to peer (2) a chirp
11. _ _ _ _ _	(1) to pucker up (2) a bag for carrying money
12. _ _ _ _ _ _	(1) purpose or aim (2) to oppose
13. _ _ _ _ _	(1) a play's area (2) a level (3) to put on
14. _ _ _ _ _ _	(1) blemish (2) to desert
15. _ _ _ _	(1) strike repeatedly (2) skin of a fur-bearing animal
16. _ _ _ _ _	(1) a drink (2) sketch or plan (3) air current
17. _ _ _ _	(1) argument (2) a gaiterlike covering for the instep (3) expectorated
18. _ _ _ _	(1) bird of prey (2) peddle by shouting
19. _ _ _ _	(1) lower end of the leg (2) twelve inches (3) to pay
20. _ _ _ _ _	(1) extra (2) to use frugally (3) a bowling term

Bonus answers: _ _ _ and _ _ _

42. WORDS WITH MUTIPLE MEANINGS

Here are fifteen words that have at least four meanings each. See how many of these meanings you can identify. If you can't get all four meanings per word, feel free to use a dictionary. The first one is done for you.

1. call:
    (a) shout; (b) communicate by telephone; (c) an inner urging toward a religious vocation; (d) order given by a square dance leader

2. fast:

3. fret:

4. sack:

5. strike:

6. run:

7. band:

8. beat:

9. brace:

10. break:

How many more words having four or more meanings can you find?

43. THE LAST SHALL BE FIRST AND THE FIRST SHALL BE LAST

Each of these twenty-one answers is a word that begins and ends with the same letter. WOW your classmates by answering each of the questions correctly.

1. _ _ _ _ margarine

2. _ _ _ _ _ _ seed of a pod-bearing plant

3. _ _ _ _ _ _ _ inhabitant of Israel

4. _ _ _ _ backtalk

5. _ _ _ _ _ fear greatly

6. _ _ _ _ _ Eskimo canoe

7. _ _ _ _ _ _ _ biting

8. _ _ _ _ feudal landlord

9. _ _ _ _ _ _ _ _ _ day before today

10. _ _ _ _ _ _ condition of iron-poor blood

11. _ _ _ _ elevated

12. _ _ _ _ group of persons

13. _ _ _ _ _ _ to flounder

14. _ _ _ _ _ an advertisement

15. _ _ _ _ _ _ _ _ gracefulness

16. _ _ _ _ _ synthetic used in hosiery

17. _ _ _ _ _ chubby

18. _ _ _ _ _ doctrine

19. _ _ _ knife used by Eskimo women

20. _ _ _ _ _ _ _ one who banters

21. _ _ _ _ _ _ _ _ force of a moving body

44. NO IF'S, AND'S, OR BUT'S ...

You sometimes hear someone say, "I don't want to hear any if's, and's or but's about it!" The words in this activity need if's, and's, and but's to complete their spellings. Insert the correct word in the proper space.

1. a_____ : to border on

2. _____ ter: bread's mate

3. comm ____ : an order

4. de _____ : first appearance before the public

5. err _____ : a trip to carry a message

6. fals _____ y: to make false

7. gr _____ : handsome and luxurious

8. hali _____ : a type of fish

9. isl _____ : a land mass surrounded by water

10. j _____ fy: a very short time

11. l _____ e: death's opposite

12. m _____ ate: an authoritative order

13. n _____ ty: a slang word for attractive or stylish

14. offh _____: extemporaneously; without much thought; at once

15. p _____ a: a type of bear

16. qu _____ ary: a state of uncertainty

17. s _____ al: a type of footwear

18. tr _____ le: something of little importance

19. upl _____ t: to raise to a higher condition

20. wh _____ f: a faint momentary smell

© 1994 by the Center for Applied Research in Education

45. "CPTN! M CPTN!"

Don't be confused by the activity's title. It is the title of Walt Whitman's poem, " O Captain! My Captain!,"dedicated to Abraham Lincoln. Obviously, the vowels are missing. The same holds true for these seventeen words that are synonyms for the word *LEADER*. Write the correct word for leader in each space.

1. _____ C H F

2. _____ H D

3. _____ L D R

4. _____ B S S

5. _____ F R M N

6. _____ S P R R

7. _____ V R S R

8. _____ M N G R

9. _____ D N

10. _____ M S T R

11. _____ M T V T R

12. _____ D R C T R

13. _____ C N D C T R

14. _____ S P R V S R

15. _____ P R N C P L

16. _____ C M M N D R

17. _____ S P R N T N D N T

46. THE DENTS THAT COST

Poor Crash Williams! He had just crashed his car into the wall and realized he would have to speak to his insurance agent about the accident. To find out what Crash told his insurance agent when asked how the accident occurred, fill in the letters surrounding the *dents* in these words and insert the circled letters consecutively in the spaces below the last question.

1. _ _ (O)D E N T a three-pronged spear

2. _ _ (O)E N T to set line from the margin

3. (O)_ _ _D E N T the West

4. D E (O)T _ _ having to do with the teeth

5. _ (O)D E N T a rat or mouse

6. _ _ _ D E N (O) wise

7. _ _ (O)D E N T pupil

8. _ _ _ D E (O)T obvious

9. _ _ _ _ (O)E N T mishap

10. D (O)N T _ _ _ false tooth

11. _ (O)_ _ _D E N T _ _ _ decreed by divine providence

12. _ _ (O)_ D E N T dweller

13. _ _ _ _ D E N (O) event

14. _ _ (O)_ _ _ _ _D E N T _ _ above human understanding

15. _ (O)D E N T _ _ _ contract binding an apprentice to a master

16. _ _ _ _ _ (O)E N T chief executive officer

17. D E N T(O)_ (O) tooth doctor

18. _ _ _ _ _D E N T first of its kind

Here is what Crash told his insurance agent: "__ _ _ _ _ _ _ _ _ _ _ _ _ _ _ _ _ _ _ _ _ _ _ _!"

47. GOLLY GEE! THE G'S HAVE GOT IT!

The answers to this crossword puzzle all begin with the letter G. *Get going, gobble up the g's,* and *give this game a good grand slam!*

ACROSS CLUES

1. to smile broadly in pleasure
2. to twist or distort the face
4. to taunt
5. to examine for collecting information
9. to stare fiercely
10. to cut or bite bit by bit
11. to catch a quick, brief look

DOWN CLUES

1. to look suddenly or briefly
2. to look intently and steadily
3. to growl
4. to stare with the mouth open
5. to make a short, deep, hoarse sound
6. to scowl
7. to make a gurgled, muffled sound
8. to look over or view

WORD LIST

GAZE	GLIMPSE	GNAW
GAPE	GLANCE	GNARL
GIBE	GLOWER	GRIN
GLEAN	GLUG	GRIMACE
GLARE	GLOM	GRUNT

48. DOUBLE YOUR PLEASURE

While doing this activity you may feel as though you have double vision. In a sense, you do since all of the words have double letter combinations. All but four letters of the alphabet are featured here. After correctly indentifying the twenty-four words below, see if any English words have double letter j, q, w, or y. Good luck!

a. _ _ _ a a _: market place

b. _ _ _ b b _ _: a petty objection

c. _ _ c c _ _ _ _: soft-sole shoe

d. _ _ d d _ _: to pamper

e. e e _ _ _: weird

f. _ _ f f _ _: to frustrate

g. _ _ g g _ _: wrangle in bargaining

h. _ _ _ h h: a fragrant gum used in incense

i. _ _ _ i i: lines from a circle's center to circumference

k. _ _ _ _ k k _ _: Jewish festival of lights

l. _ _ _ l l: short descriptive poem about country life

m. _ _ m m _ _: instrument for driving nails

n. _ n n _ _ _: inborn

o. _ o o _ _ _: small, highly intelligent dog

p. _ _ p p _ _ _ _: well-being; joy

r. _ _ r r _: regret

s. _ _ s s _: impudent

t. _ _ _ _ t t _ _: to disparage

u. _ _ _ u u _: void

v. _ _ v v _: know-how

x. _ x x _ _: an oil company

z. _ _ z z _: giddy; lightheaded

49. DROP THAT LETTER RIGHT NOW!

Here are fifteen pairs of words that have something in common. The first word in each pair has one more letter than the second word since a letter has been dropped to form the pair's second word. Identify both words in the pair by their definitions. The first pair is done for you.

1. w i l d e r   less civilized
   w i d e r   broader

2. _ _ _ _ _   support for a broken arm
   _ _ _ _   vocalize musically

3. _ _ _ _ _ _   cultivator
   _ _ _ _ _   strength

4. _ _ _ _   sluggish
   _ _ _   adult female pig

5. _ _ _ _ _   a menacing sound
   _ _ _ _   develop

6. _ _ _ _   engage in recreation
   _ _ _   give what is due

7. _ _ _ _ _ _   smallest amount
   _ _ _ _   a direction

8. _ _ _ _ _   a tag
   _ _ _ _   a Biblical figure

9. _ _ _ _   to wither
   _ _ _   one who comes out with clever remarks

10. _ _ _ _ _   blasé
    _ _ _ _   group of musicians

11. _ _ _ _   happiness
    _ _ _   exclamation of surprise

12. _ _ _ _ _   hard rock
    _ _ _ _   to satisfy

13. _ _ _ _   a group having common ancestry
    _ _ _   has the ability

14. _ _ _ _ _   hard outer covering
    _ _ _ _   opposite of heaven

15. _ _ _ _ _ _   one who exhales
    _ _ _ _ _   opposite of higher

50. I'LL DRINK TO THAT!

‿༼෴༽‿

Match these twenty words that contain the word ADE in them. Hidden within the letters that make up the correct answer key is a famous author. Can you find him?

1. ___ charade
2. ___ arcade
3. ___ blockade
4. ___ brigade
5. ___ adept
6. ___ facade
7. ___ decade
8. ___ adequate
9. ___ lade
10. ___ parade
11. ___ wade
12. ___ shade
13. ___ blade
14. ___ invade
15. ___ made
16. ___ evade
17. ___ bade
18. ___ cadence
19. ___ grade
20. ___ fade

a. military unit
b. step through water
c. created
d. guessing game or pretense
e. public procession
f. grow dim
g. express a greeting
h. the cutting part of the tool
i. front of a building
j. passage with arched roof
k. strategic barrier
l. variety of a color
m. elude
n. degree or stage
o. to dip or draw out
p. sufficient
q. proficient
r. ten years
s. forcibly enter
t. rhythm

Who is the famous author found in the answers? _____

51. HOW PROUD!

Six words that are synonyms for the word *proud* are found in this word grid. The letters of each word must be in a box adjacent to each other. All 36 letters in the grid will be used, but no box will be used twice. The word *vain* has already been found for you. Find the other five words and write the words below the grid.

D	N	P	D	I	F
A	I	L	Y	E	S
L	A	E	C	K	I
G	V	A	O	C	T
D	E	S	T	N	A
C	O	N	T	E	S

_____ VAIN _____ _____

_____ _____

_____ _____

52. WORDS WORTH THEIR WEIGHT IN GOLD

The chemical element GOLD has the chemcial symbol Au. The abbreviation is from the Latin word aurum meaning gold. Below are twenty-five words containing the "golden combination," au. Match the words from the list with their proper definitions.

applause	*august*	*beau*	*gaudy*	*paucity*
auction	*auk*	*bureau*	*hautboy*	*raucous*
audience	*aura*	*caught*	*jaunty*	*rondeau*
augment	*austere*	*daub*	*laud*	*tableau*
augury	*bauxite*	*daughter*	*naughty*	*taut*

1. _____ captured
2. _____ praise
3. _____ female offspring
4. _____ smear
5. _____ oboe
6. _____ invisible emanation
7. _____ sea bird
8. _____ increase
9. _____ tight
10. _____ spectators
11. _____ scarcity
12. _____ harsh
13. _____ stern
14. _____ venerable
15. _____ stylish
16. _____ omen
17. _____ garish
18. _____ public sale
19. _____ disobedient
20. _____ claylike ore
21. _____ clapping of hands
22. _____ short, lyrical poem
23. _____ striking scene or picture
24. _____ suitor
25 _____ dresser or chest of drawers

How many more words with the au combination can you think of?

© 1994 by the Center for Applied Research in Education

53. LUCKY SEVENS

Here is an exercise that tests your knowledge of seven letter words. Every answer has seven letters. Fill in the words that fit each definition and have some fun with Lucky Seven's.

PUZZLE 1

Across

1. burned with hot liquid

2. a feeling of high regard

Down

1. a plotter

3. one-celled microscopic organisms

5. to dislike intensely

7. extinct

PUZZLE 2

Across

1. a rich cloth with a raised design

2. to wreck

Down

1. hallowed

3. threatening

5. one who asserts without proof

7. ambassador's residency

54. SILENT FIRST LETTERS

How many of these thirteen words that begin with silent letters can you identify? PSYCHE yourself up for this activity in which silence speaks loudly!

© 1994 by the Center for Applied Research in Education

ACROSS CLUES

2. to make by looping thread together
3. the joint of the leg
4. science of human and animal behavior
9. a chronic skin disease
10. an African antelope
11. incorrect
12. to inscribe
13. a plant used as a medicine

DOWN CLUES

1. a memory device
4. and illness associated with the lungs
5. high regard
6. dwarflike creature
7. an emperor
8. a false name
9. an alkaloid substance that may be poisonous

WORD LIST

CZAR	HERB	KNIT	PSEUDONYM	PTOMAINE
GNOME	HONOR	MNEMONIC	PSORIASIS	WRITE
GNU	KNEE	PNEUMONIA	PSYCHOLOGY	WRONG

55. YOU WILL START IT . . . U WILL END IT

All of these twenty words end with the letter U. Locate the defined word within the maze and then write the word next to its definition. The words are placed backwards, forward, diagonally, and up and down. The first one is done for you.

```
F N Z V Z M Q Z L T X B Z C B X X Q D V G S P M
H D L D P K B H U D M J X D R F M V C N Q Y N P
K K L N G W C L P O P A H T N B Y L M W G G T R
N P L S B T P K T C B D N R B C T N G P A W L H
U R R T J N D C J Y T I H T M B G W Z D G L B S
R E S X A Q G C G T L P R Y E H P U I D V L L V
L W I Z S B S N D C S X L A Z A Z E R P E R L U
F A B L I A U E L B A T E C R U E M U L F T C
Z T R W I F L R Q W B P K M Z A Y A K C E U S P
Z Y K B A M N Z E H S L T J E Q G I E J T I W N
L F Y N P C T B D A H C J B Q D A X N D V R L X
V S S Y B P R P S F U S Z G D H G B M T N C M W
W J V Q Q Y H X W M T R V C D R B H Q J F O N N
Q Z Y S J T Z G J N C Z C H P F X D B F S S R G
F T B Q W Q B V W Y J F X G Z T Q N C G L C B K
W D Q D G Q V D N Q N C C S C J S T Z W X P G T
W C B B K J H X D N G K P R K V C K N M H B M C
```

1. <u>haiku</u>   Japanese style of poetry

2. _____ a type of cheese

3. _____ beige

4. _____ cloak

5. _____ colloquial for virus

6. _____ dresser

7. _____ goodbye

8. _____ large African antelope

9. _____ large North American reindeer

10. _____ large, flightless bird

11. _____ mishap

12. _____ place; stead

13. _____ sacred prohibition

14. _____ short ballet apparel

15. _____ short story in verse

16. _____ short, lyrical poem

17. _____ social or cultural setting

18. _____ spiritual advisor

19. _____ striking dramatic scene

20. _____ suitor

Section III

The World Around You

Name _____   Date _____   Period _____

56. THE HUMAN BODY

Listed below are twenty body parts. These words should be inserted in the correct blanks to correctly identify the defined words. Once you have filled in the correct letters, unscramble the circled letters to identify three other body parts not on this list. Each body part on this list is used only once.

ankle	ear	head	knee	lip	neck	toe
arm	face	heel	knuckle	liver	rib	tooth
chin	hand	hip	leg	mouth	shin	

1. W _____ circular frame

2. _____ SOME palatable

3. _____ E to polish

4. C _____ PER in good spirits

5. _____ ISTICE agreed temporary stopping of warfare

6. _____ L to bend with the knees in church or elsewhere

7. UR _____ a roguish youngster

8. MISTLE _____ women standing beneath it might get kissed

9. _____ NEST serious

10. AL _____ ATION assertion

11. F _____ PANT impertinent

12. _____ LONG recklessly

13. DE _____ mar

14. S _____ a small piece

15. LITTLE _____ a type of clam

16. _____ SOME good looking

17. _____ HEAD a stupid person

18. VER _____ a sweet or dry white wine

19. R _____ D caused long-lasting anger

20. D _____ BLE to bounce a ball

The three other body parts found in the circled letters are: __ __ __ __ __ __   __ __ __ __
__ __ __ __.

57. BODY PARTS MAZE

How many body parts of three or more letters can you find in this word maze? Start with a letter and use any letter touching it to construct the names of as many body parts as you can. You may use a single letter consecutively to form words with double letters such as heel. Twelve body parts or more makes you a champion in this game.

K	O	S	L	K
C	N	E	A	N
E	Y	H	L	T
M	R	E	O	U
W	A	T	G	M
J	D	X	U	S

_____   _____   _____

_____   _____   _____

_____   _____   _____

_____   _____   _____

_____   _____   _____

58. WORDS YOU CAN TASTE

For some strange reason we like to include food in our daily language. How many of the following names and expressions associated with food can you identify?

1. An _____ a day keeps the doctor away.

2. ...a partridge in a _____ tree.

3. Miami's _____ Bowl

4. a boxer's deformed ear is called a _____ ear

5. a poorly performing car is called a_____

6. a high paying job that requires little work is called a _____

7. Lorraine Hansberry's play is called A _____ in the Sun

8. a sourpuss is a real _____

9. to force one's way in is to _____ in

10. a politically unstable Latin American country is referred to as a _____ republic

11. a growth on your toe is a _____

12. a social engagement is a _____

13. a redheaded person is called a _____ top

14. an _____ branch is a symbol of peace.

15. preseason baseball is called the _____ league

16. a small person is called a _____

17. a dumb person is referred to as a _____ or a _____

18. paper money is called _____

19. a showoff is a _____ - _____

20. one who shows little courage is a _____

21. a tall, skinny person is a _____ _____

22. a person who is well-liked is a _____

23. in old slang an attractive woman was a _____

24. to be in a difficult situation is to be in a_____

25. a gentle or innocent person is called a_____

Can you think of more expressions or situations involving foods? Share them with your classmates.

59. WORDS GOOD ENOUGH TO EAT

How many foods consisting of three or more letters can you find in this maze? Start with a letter and use any letter touching it to construct the names of as many foods as you can. Use a single letter twice to form double letters as in jelly. Finding twelve or more foods makes you an expert in the AMAZING activity. (Puns are always welcomed here!)

M	A	L	I	A	Y
J	L	P	K	M	P
Y	E	R	A	E	G
D	N	O	E	G	A
A	C	W	S	T	D

_____   _____   _____

_____   _____   _____

_____   _____   _____

_____   _____   _____

_____   _____   _____

_____   _____   _____

60. MATCH THEIR MATES

Tom Doe, the careless zoologist, has a problem. He has brought forty animals to the zoo, but he has somehow mixed up all the females. Help Tom match the females with their male counterparts by writing the correct answers in the spaces. The word cow will be used three times and the word doe will be used twice.

cow (3)	ewe	hen	mare	queen	tigress
doe (2)	female	jenny	nanny	she-bear	vixen
duck	goose	lioness	pen	sow	

ANIMAL	MALE	FEMALE
1. bear	he-bear	_____
2. cat	tom	_____
3. cattle	bull	_____
4. chicken	rooster	_____
5. deer	buck	_____
6. donkey	jack	_____
7. duck	drake	_____
8. elephant	bull	_____
9. fox	dog	_____
10. goat	billy	_____
11. goose	gander	_____
12. horse	stallion	_____
13. lion	lion	_____
14. monkey	male	_____
15. rabbit	buck	_____
16. sheep	ram	_____
17. swan	cob	_____
18. swine	boar	_____
19. tiger	tiger	_____
20. whale	bull	_____

61. FERRET OUT THESE ANSWERS!

The names of various animals can be used to describe actions or conditions in life. To lionize someone is to treat that person as you would a celebrity. Show your animal instincts by matching these expressions with the correct animals.

1. ___ ape
2. ___ bear
3. ___ buffalo
4. ___ chicken
5. ___ cow
6. ___ crab
7. ___ crow
8. ___ dog's life
9. ___ duck
10. ___ fish
11. ___ horse
12. ___ mouse
13. ___ pigeonhole
14. ___ piggyback
15. ___ rat
16. ___ seal
17. ___ skunk
18. ___ squirrel
19. ___ weasel
20. ___ whale of a time

a. to close completely
b. to bluff
c. to keep from scoring any points
d. afraid
e. to store or hoard
f. to intimidate
g. exceptionally great
h. on the shoulders
i. wretched existence
j. to mimic
k. to put up with
l. to inform on
m. to classify
n. to complain
o. to avoid a task
p. hand-held computer device
q. try to get something indirectly
r. to boast in triumph
s. to fool around
t. a sneaky person

© 1994 by the Center for Applied Research in Education

Write a story using any ten of these animal words as defined in the matching column.

62. A BAND OF GORILLAS

~~~

Familiarize yourself with the group names of these twenty animals. Write the group name next to its appropriate animal name.

band   flock   pack   swarm
bed   gaggle   pod   tribe
colony   herd   pride   troop
covey   leap   school   watch
exaltation litter   skulk   yoke

1. _____ quail   11. _____ monkeys

2. _____ leopards   12. _____ bees

3. _____ foxes   13. _____ goats

4. _____ oxen   14. _____ sheep

5. _____ gorillas   15. _____ geese

6. _____ larks   16. _____ ants

7. _____ elephants   17. _____ nightingales

8. _____ lions   18. _____ whales

9. _____ fish   19. _____ hounds

10. _____ clams   20. _____ pigs

63. FOR THE BIRDS

Here are the scrambled names of forty-four birds. Write their correct spellings in the space next to the bird.

1. _____ ahkw

2. _____ cenar

3. _____ kua

4. _____ aarcny

5. _____ dtraicb

6. _____ ienglnaithg

7. _____ aelge

8. _____ acdrnila

9. _____ low

10. _____ akrl

11. _____ udrebilb

12. _____ ocpkrdeewo

13. _____ ocookwcd

14. _____ cowr

15. _____ eovdilrb

16. _____ ancflo

17. _____ eum

18. _____ ialuq

19. _____ ulgl

20. _____ ohorwwlplipi

21. _____ glnrtisa

22. _____ ghitanhkw

23. _____ tnre

24. _____ aegdpirtr

25. _____ psroawr

26. _____ rnwe

27. _____ lreoio

28. _____ vaoect

29. _____ ukytre

30. _____ tskor

31. _____ toco

32. _____ bacbrildk

33. _____ onirb

34. _____ hccikeade

35. _____ arrtop

36. _____ gnioep

37. _____ onol

38. _____ ruuetvl

39. _____ wwoslal

40. _____ asdprnepi

41. _____ druigbnhimm

42. _____ kgndcriibom

43. _____ csiohrt

44. _____ ihnmecy sitwf

64. THE PARADE OF INSTRUMENTS

Kate, the confused conductor, has mixed up the various instruments of the orchestra. Help Kate get the orchestra back in working order by unscrambling each instrument's name and then writing that instrument's name and its type in the space provided.

The types of instruments are:

Woodwinds (W): wind instruments made especially of wood

Strings (S): instruments usually made of wood with tones produced by vibrating string

Percussion (P): an instrument whose sound is produced by striking or rattling the instrument

Brass (B): wind instruments made of coiled metal tubes and usually having a cup-shaped mouthpiece

1. <u>bassoon W</u> abnooss
2. _____ ltceanir
3. _____ Fhrcne hnro
4. _____ Ehgsinl hnor
5. _____ dsrmu
6. _____ assb cetnlira
7. _____ flteu
8. _____ icopclo
9. _____ beoo
10. _____ niilov
11. _____ leolc
12. _____ sabs
13. _____ xheonployc
14. _____ smlaybc
15. _____ lrtiaeng
16. _____ rnteoobm
17. _____ osuaespnoh

65. A WORLD OF NATIONS

Fill in the following blanks with the appropriate nationality. Nationalities may be used more than once. The first one is done for you.

1. <u>French</u> fries

2. Great _____

3. Ugly _____

4. _____ treat

5. _____ muffins

6. _____ nut

7. _____ knit sweater

8. _____ man-of-war

9. _____ bacon

10. _____ waffles

11. _____ goulash

12. _____ roulette

13. _____ Guards

14. _____ shepherd

15. _____ ink

16. _____ checkers

17. _____ Corridor

18. _____ Steps in Rome

19. _____ meatballs

20. _____ bread

21. _____ rug

22. _____ soda bread

23. _____ urn

24. _____ beetle

25. _____ baths

26. _____ coffee

27. _____ toast

66. THE ROADS THAT ARE TAKEN

A word from Robert Frost's memorable poem, "The Road Not Taken," is the way to go here since you are asked to find the nineteen different types of *roads* hidden in the cryptograms below. Write the correct answers in the spaces provided. Happy trails!

1. _____ V P D L Q C X Z

2. _____ S C R S U Y J

3. _____ D H V Y D J

4. _____ F Y L Z

5. _____ K V D Z Z V

6. _____ E J Q Y K K

7. _____ A H P D V

8. _____ E H P F Z W Y D T

9. _____ T D C W Z

10. _____ Y D V Z D J

11. _____ Q Y D X U Y J

12. _____ Z I Q D Z K K U Y J

13. _____ D H P V Z

14. _____ Y W Z L P Z

15. _____ V S D P U Y J

16. _____ K Z D W C A Z   D H Y T

17. _____ A Y P K Z U Y J

18. _____ N D Z Z U Y J

19. _____ V S H D H P R S N Y D Z

Real letters: A B C D E F G H I J K L M N O P Q R S T U V W X Y Z

Substitute letters: Y _ _ _ _ _ _ _ _ _ _ _ _ _ _ _ _ _ _ _ K _ _ _ _ _

© 1994 by the Center for Applied Research in Education

67. PLACES IN NAMES

⤷ ∾⤶

All of the following described persons have cities, states or countries as either their first, middle or last name. See how well you combine your knowledge of people and geography.

1. Jack _____ author of *The Sea Wolf*

2. Michael _____ basketball star

3. _____ O'Keeffe artist

4. Anatole _____ Nobel winning French author

5. Joe _____ football quarterback

6. John _____ singer and actor

7. Whitney _____ pop singer

8. Michael _____ pop singer

9. Grover _____ U.S. President

10. Rick _____ pop singer

11. Tony _____ singer

12. George _____ U.S. President

13. _____ Brontë British author of *Jane Eyre*

14. Sir Walter _____ explorer

15. _____ Dukakis actress

16. _____ Trudeau Canadian political leader

17. James _____ U.S. President

18. D.H. _____ British author

19. John _____ author of *Paradise Lost*

20. Katherine _____ British short story writer

21. John Greenleaf _____ American poet

22. _____ O'Neill American dramatist

23. William _____ wrote *The Death of a President*

24. Amy _____ American poetess

25. Douglas _____ American swashbuckling actor

How many more examples can you recall? Write them down and challenge your classmates.

68. THE STATES' ABBREVIATIONS *(PART ONE)*

Below are the abbreviations (in alphabetical order) of twenty-four states. Each has been placed within a word whose definition is also given. Identify the state by writing it after the clue and then identify the defined word.

1. _ A L _ _ _ _   a unit of mesuring heat _____
2. _ A K _   a garden tool _____
3. A Z _ _ _   blue _____
4. _ A R _ _ _   trade _____
5. C A _ _ _ _ _ _ _   disaster _____
6. C O _ _ _ _   chemical element used in paint _____
7. _ _ _ _ _ _ C T   short and to the point _____
8. D E _ _ _ _   item _____
9. F L _ _ _   a baking ingredient _____
10. G A _ _   to look at intently _____
11. _ H I _ _   a sound made by a bird _____
12. _ I D _ _ _   a puzzle _____
13. _ I L _ _ _   a device used to catch impurities _____
14. I N _ _ _ _   a blue dye _____
15. _ I A _ _   a thing of superhuman size _____
16. _ _ _ K S _ _ _ _   a short metal bar attached to a bicycle _____
17. _ _ _ K Y   gloomy _____
18. _ L A _ _ _   pestilence _____
19. _ _ _ _ M E   a crafty plot _____
20. _ M D _ _ _ _ _   a city in Sudan _____
21. _ M A _ _   to break into pieces _____
22. _ _ M I _ _ _ _   to lessen _____
23. _ _ M N   to condemn _____
24. _ _ _ M S   cars in the mines _____

69. THE STATES' ABBREVIATIONS (PART TWO)

Below are the abbreviations (in alphabetical order) of twenty-four states. Each has been placed within a word whose definition is also given. Identify the state by writing it after the clue and then identify the defined word.

1. M O _ _ _ _ _   force of a moving body _____

2. _ M T _ _ _   U.S. train system _____

3. _ N E _ _   genuflect _____

4. _ N V _ _ _   enter with force _____

5. _ N H _ _ _   breathe in _____

6. _ N J _ _ _   to hurt _____

7. _ N M _ _ _   prisoner _____

8. _ _ _ N Y   black _____

9. _ N C _   one-twelfth of a foot _____

10. _ N D _ _ _ _ _   an earnest attempt _____

11. _ O H _ _ _ _ _   sticking together _____

12. _ O K _ _   a symbol _____

13. _ O R _ _ _ _   piece _____

14. _ P A _ _ _ _   relating to space _____

15. R I _ _ _ _ _ _   to deride _____

16. _ _ S C _ _ _ _   trouble _____

17. _ _ S D _ _ _ _ _ _   to manage incorrectly _____

18. _ _ _ _ T N _ _ _   mental acuity _____

19. _ U T _ _ _   flesh of sheep _____

20. _ _ V T   the abbreviation for government _____

21. V A _ _ _ _ _   a substance used to prevent disease _____

22. W A _ _   a homeless child _____

23. W I _ _   to hope for _____

24. _ _ _ W Y   full of snow _____

Name _____ Date _____ Period _____

70. LITTLE VENICE IN SOUTH AMERICA

The origins of cities' and countries' names can be interesting. Did you know that Venezuela really means Little Venice? Start with that answer and move on to other interesting geographical names' origins.

1. ___ Andes   a. black pool

2. ___ Brooklyn   b. the north-way

3. ___ Chicago   c. young cattle

4. ___ Detroit   d. sanctuary

5. ___ Dublin   e. metal

6. ___ Greenland   f. hair people

7. ___ Holland   g. new land

8. ___ Italy   h. South Slavs

9. ___ Japan   i. tree or stump projecting out of the water

10. ___ Los Angeles   j. killers

11. ___ Mecca   k. water-course through a swamp

12. ___ Norway   l. three cities

13. ___ Ottawa   m. the bold ones

14. ___ Paris   n. wild onion place

15. ___ Pensacola   o. Little Venice

16. ___ Toronto   p. straight, narrows

17. ___ Tripoli   q. Queen of the Angels

18. ___ Venezuela   r. place of the sun's origin

19. ___ Yosemite   s. boiling

20. ___ Yugoslavia   t. woodland

71. THE SPORTING LIFE

How well do you know your sports terminology? Prove your sports knowledge by matching these twenty terms with their correct sports. Then use the circled letters to identify another sports term. Each of the twenty answers is used only once.

TERM

1. ___ balk
2. ___ touchdown
3. ___ shuttlecock
4. ___ blue line
5. ___ slam dunk
6. ___ bull's-eye
7. ___ ground stroke
8. ___ sweeper
9. ___ half nelson
10. ___ eagle
11. ___ crop
12. ___ win, place, show
13. ___ pit crew
14. ___ breast stroke
15. ___ marathon
16. ___ setter
17. ___ gainer
18. ___ parallel bars
19. ___ scaling
20. ___ gutter ball

SPORT

a. hockey
b. wrestling
c. equestrian
d. swimming
e. soccer
f. auto racing
g. badminton
h. golf
i. bowling
j. baseball
k. running
l. basketball
m. horse racing
n. football
o. diving
p. mountain climbing
q. archery
r. gymnastics
s. volleyball
t. tennis

The circled letters answer this question. Which sport is known as the SPORT OF KINGS?

_____

72. A TREE IS A TREE IS A TREE?

Gertrude Stein, the author who made famous the line, "A rose is a rose is a rose," would enjoy this activity. By changing one letter in the names of these eighteen trees listed in Column A, a new word's definition is listed in Column B. Thus *ash* matches up with *snake* since an *asp* is a *snake*. The first one is already done for you. List the new word after the definition in Column B.

Hint: Most of the new words will rhyme with the words listed in the first column.

COLUMN A

1. _h_ ash

2. ___ aspen

3. ___ beech

4. ___ birch

5. ___ cherry

6. ___ coffee

7. ___ date

8. ___ elm

9. ___ holly

10. ___ lime

11. ___ mango

12. ___ oak

13. ___ palm

14. ___ pine

15. ___ plum

16. ___ teak

17. ___ willow

18. ___ yew

COLUMN B

a. South American dance _____

b. happy _____

c. pallid _____

d. cushion _____

e. summit _____

f. tardy _____

g. foolishness _____

h. snake ___ asp ___

i. creation _____

j. a small number _____

k. half a quart _____

l. paddle _____

m. peaceful _____

n. bloodsucking worm _____

o. candy _____

p. sprite _____

q. sullen _____

r. duration _____

73. THE FOUR MATH OPERATIONS

Sixteen words that contain the abbreviations for the four math operations are the answers to this crossword puzzle. Fill in the correct answers.

ACROSS CLUES

1. using habitually
5. sacred
8. father
9. to rent to another
11. noisy commotion
12. an addition to
13. toddle
15. legal dissolution of a marriage
16. a cultivated, lettucelike plant

DOWN CLUES

2. a unit
3. cannot be divided
4. soft material
6. a large number of persons
7. wildly excited
10. seeking to overthrow
14. different

74. THE WORLD OF MATHEMATICS

Twelve math terms are defined below. Fill in the missing letters. Then by unscrambling the circled letters, identify two other math terms. Write the two terms beneath the last question.

1. _ θ _ _ _ _ θ _: a three-sided figure

2. _ _ _ _ _ θ _ _: the quantity to be divided

3. θ _ _ _ θ _ _: round figures

4. _ θ _ _ θ _: a line from the circle's center to the periphery

5. _ _ _ θ _ _: a symbol or word showing how many

6. θ _ _ _ _ _ _ _: branch of math dealing with points, lines, and planes

7. _ _ _ θ _: the shape made by two straight lines meeting at a point

8. θ _ _ _ _ _ _ _: similarity of arrangement

9. _ θ _ _ _: the quotient of one quantity divided by another of the same kind

10. θ _ _ _ _ _ _ _: the adding of two or more numbers to get a sum

11. _ _ _ _ _ _ _ _ _ θ :   the science of computing with real numbers

12. _ _ _ _ _ _ _ θ _ _: the longest side of a right triangle

The two other math terms are: _____ and _____.

75. A NUMBER OF THINGS

How well do you know what makes up what? Certainly you know that there are seven days in a week and four quarters in a dollar. Such information in this exercise would be written "7 = D. in a W." and "4 = Q. in a D." How many more of these can you figure out? Write your answers in the spaces provided.

1. _____ 365 1/4 = D. in a Y.

2. _____ 50 = U.S.S.

3. _____ 4 = Q. in a G.

4. _____ 10 = P. in a D.

5. _____ 7 = W. of the A. W.

6. _____ 101 = D.

7. _____ 30 = D. hath S.

8. _____ 4 = S. in a Y.

9. _____ 1001 = A.K.

10. _____ 435 = M. of the H. of R.

11. _____ 7 = O. of the W.

12. _____ 3 = B. M. (S.H.T.R.)

13. _____ 95 = T. of M. L.

14. _____ 1492 = Y. C. S. the O. B.

15. _____ 10 = D. in a D.

16. _____ 3 = F. in a Y.

17. _____ 10 = K. in 6.2 M.

18. _____ 5280 = F. in a M.

19. _____ 8 = P. of S.

20. _____ 88 = K. on a P.

© 1994 by the Center for Applied Research in Education

Name _____ **Date** _____ **Period** _____

76. LAND FORMATIONS

Twenty-six land formations are hidden in the word find below. Circle the answers that are placed backwards, forward, diagonally, and up and down. The first one is done for you.

```
J B B T C B J K W D K N W T N T P L K G Q P K B
S S W Q H C H M B M L C K M L H Y K D G H L K K
Y X V S C W O X F C Q C M U S N A X Z G F W P Y
C H A S M G O R G E L E A P L A I N R E V A C C
M K I Y U P U P A F G E B R L C V A N M T T B S
T D R L J M S L S V T S Q F R C A I T A B T B B
V V A P L T E K L A I K C H A O A N D N V T U D
V A L L E Y B S L Y F N C M R R Y B Y L U A T B
Y F L P E I P P A H K L E O O F D O C O Y O S B
Y Q P E R H R J V B U A J M L M R N R D N C M S
L E G Z X P K I M G D L H P S L J G U H S C N Y
C H N H V B S J A O Q Z M D T Z I W N T B F Y T
M N H H V H S F W R R P X Z V K J H D H K G Z M
C C C T N N Q K Q Z P G F V G N F V J P Y T W B
C X K Z N C J H Z V V M H K N Y G G G R F H M H
V N S W S T Z Z T F H G Z D G J L Z Y G N T R C
M K B H C L B M H Z W Y C C B H N R X W K M Q W
```

ARROYO	GULCH	MOGUL	SAVANNA
BUTTE	GULLY	MORAINE	STEPPE
CANYON	HILL	MOUNTAIN	TUNDRA
CAVERN	HILLOCK	PLAIN	VALE
CHASM	LEA	PLATEAU	VALLEY
DALE	MEADOW	PRAIRIE	
GORGE	MESA	RAVINE	

77. IT'S ELEMENTARY, MY DEAR WATSON!

Using your knowledge of chemical elements, identify the defined word by using the symbols of the elements found after the definition. Fill in the elements' names as well. A few letters are there to help you. Assume all the letters in the elements' symbols are capital letters. The first one is done for you.

1. F E A R: apprehension ____iron____ + ____argon____

2. C _ _ G: a steep, rugged rock projecting from a rock mass _____ + _____

3. _ _ N _: a sheet of glass _____ + _____

4. C _ _ N _: to make a copy of _____ + _____ + _____

5. _ E _ R: alcoholic beverage made from grain _____ + _____

6. _ A I _: to increase _____ + _____ + _____

7. _ E _ R: close _____ + _____

8. _ U T _: pretty or attractive _____ + _____

9. _ _ S: a fuel _____ + _____

10. B R _ _ _: a clear, thin soup made by boiling meat _____ + _____ + _____

11. C _ A _: substance found in mines _____ + _____

12. _ _ C _: ill _____ + _____ + _____

13. B _ _ _: prejudice _____ + _____

14. L _ _ K: fortune _____ + _____ + _____

15. X _ _ _ _ _ _ B _: one who fears foreigners _____ + _____ + _____ + _____ + _____ + _____ + _____

© 1994 by the Center for Applied Research in Education

Name _____ Date _____ Period _____

78. IT'S ALL IN THE STARS!

Here's an exercise that will have you seeing stars! The names of twenty constellations provide the answers to this crossword puzzle. So whether you're a Pisces or a Gemini, have fun with this puzzle!

ACROSS CLUES

1. Wolf
6. the Sea-goat
7. Chained Maiden
9. Scorpion
11. Ram
12. Twins
14. Maiden
15. Swan
16. Archer
17. Little Dog
18. Queen

DOWN CLUES

2. Fishes
3. Bull
4. Balance or Scales
5. Lion
6. Crab
7. Water Bearer
8. Dove
10. Flying Horse
13. Great Bear

WORD LIST

ANDROMEDA	COLUMBA	PISCES
AQUARIUS	CYGNUS	SAGITTARIUS
ARIES	GEMINI	SCORPIO
CANCER	LEO	TAURUS
CANISMINOR	LIBRA	URSAMAJOR
CAPRICORN	LUPUS	VIRGO
CASSIOPEIA	PEGASUS	

79. SIZING UP YOUR SCIENCE SENSE

Do you know the difference between botany and zoology? Between geology and ecology? Here's your chance to shine! Write the correct answers to these clues all dealing with sciences.

© 1994 by the Center for Applied Research in Education

ACROSS CLUES

5. rocks and earthquakes
9. plant and animal fossils
10. environment
11. function of living things
12. language
13. elements and substances and their properties

DOWN CLUES

1. atmosphere and weather
2. plants
3. brain
4. human beings' origin and culture
6. animals
7. stars and planets
8. drugs
11. matter and energy

WORD LIST

ANTHROPOLGY
ASTRONOMY
BOTANY
CHEMISTRY
ECOLOGY

GEOLOGY
LINGUISTICS
METEOROLOGY
PALEONTOLOGY
PHARMACOLOGY

PHYSICS
PHYSIOLOGY
PSYCHOLOGY
ZOOLOGY

80. A MEATY ISSUE

All the words in this list are meats. Find the letters that were substituted in the original word. A list of letters is at the bottom to help you along.

1. S T A O

2. P U X E H   J V V Q

3. E H V X O

4. E X T E X F V

5. Z X D J

6. H T P O V W

7. A I Y A O V L

8. J X A U L

9. Z Y C V P

10. Q Y Z V H   D Y F L U L

11. C V X Z

12. I U H   S U F

13. Q P V E I   I X D

14. I X D

15. M U P O

16. C V L Y E U L

17. H V L S V P Z U Y L

1. _ _ _ _

2. _ _ _ _ _   _ _ _

3. _ _ _ _ _

4. _ _ _ _ _ _ _

5. _ _ _ _

6. _ _ _ _ _ _

7. _ _ _ _ _ _ _

8. _ _ _ _ _

9. _ _ _ _ _

10. _ _ _ _ _   _ _ _ _ _ _

11. _ _ _ _

12. _ _ _   _ _ _

13. _ _ _ _ _   _ _ _

14. _ _ _

15. _ _ _ _

16. _ _ _ _ _ _ _

17. _ _ _ _ _ _ _ _ _

Letter: A B C D E F G H I J K L M N O P Q R S T U V W X Y Z

Substitute: _ _ _ _ <u>V</u> _ _ _ _ _ _ _ _ _ <u>L</u> _ _ _ _ _ _ _ _ _ _ _

81. THE PRESIDENTS' ROUNDUP

The last names of twenty-five U.S. Presidents are hidden in this word find puzzle. After you have found the names of each man, write his first name in the space next to his last name.

All words in this list are associated with U.S. Presidents. The words are placed backwards, forward, diagonally, up and down. The names below the word searches can help you find the words. The first one is already done for you.

```
P R B Z T P M T S R T V G T N Z S W H W T N L G
R G E X W R S B N W V L H K Q A M E V N Y M G N
N F X T M J U M R A R A L K L D N X Y Y M R X N
R U H T R A G M D E R O M L L I F A D A M S R M
X E K Q H A A B A R P G L E J D N E H Z H E M N
K W A R R D C V I N D Y I Y Q E N C S C L Q F Q
T N A G I D J S X N G F P N A N F C O Y U W T N
C Z C S A N O O E F R D O T E T H F T L B B M S
V N O W H N J R H A J S Z K G M T S E Z N S Z D
Z N F L K I U T G N K G F Y B B B S V R T J K W
G R P N D B N E Q C S M B U S H Z R Q Z S L P Z
V C D I N Q O G A D X O H Q G W L D K P S O K G
K Q K A E R Q J T F Y T N H R G J G L W F B N F
L K V D N R P X G O R V Y F M H R R K Z H K L D
T T L O Q K C F Z K N G Q R H G B R T N M G V C
C K M D B V C E X T Q X G V Y M P R T M M L C F
K G J Q Q P Q L G B N P M C K D G W F X K D H T
```

John Adams   _____ Grant   _____ Lincoln   _____ Truman
_____ Arthur   _____ Harrison   _____ Madison   _____ Tyler
_____ Buchanan   _____ Hayes   _____ Monroe   _____ VanBuren
_____ Bush   _____ Jackson   _____ Pierce   _____ Washington
_____ Carter   _____ Jefferson   _____ Polk
_____ Fillmore   _____ Johnson   _____ Reagan
_____ Garfield   _____ Kennedy   _____ Taylor

82. THE UNITED STATES

⚬⚭⚬

Twenty of our fifty states have been scrambled up next to their nicknames. Unscramble the states, write their names in the appropriate spaces, and then using the circled letters, identify four states that were not used in the first twenty.

STATES	SCRAMBLED STATES	STATES' NICKNAMES
1. _ _ _ Ø _ _	aaskla	The Last Frontier
2. _ _ _ _ Ø _ _ _	mnhgacii	The Great Lake State
3. _ _ _ _ Ø	suhot caoainlr	Palmetto State
_ _ _ Ø _ _ _ _		
4. _ _ _ _ _ _	erngoo	Beaver State
5. Ø _ _ _ _ _ _ _ _	siwcninso	Badger State
6. _ _ _ _ _ _ _ Ø _ _	clfaoaniir	Golden State
7. _ _ _ _ _ _ Ø _ _	wen eejysr	Garden State
8. _ Ø _ _ _ _ _ _	earaksbn	Cornhusker State
9. _ _ _ _ Ø _ Ø	tannaom	Treasure State
10. _ _ _ _ _ _ _	islonili	The Prairie State
11. _ _ Ø _ _ _ _	laaaabm	Heart of Dixie
12. _ _ _ Ø _ _ _ _	wdearlae	First State
13. Ø _ Ø _ _ _ _ _	ynkcuetk	Bluegrass State
14. _ _ _ _ Ø _ _	raodilf	Sunshine State
15. _ _ _ _ Ø _ _	nwe roky	Empire State
16. _ _ _ _ _ _ Ø _	kamaoohl	Sooner State
17. _ _ _ _ _ Ø _ _	oalordoc	Centennial State
18. _ _ _ _ _	xeast	Lone Star State
19. _ _ _ Ø _ _ _ _ _	anaiosliu	Pelican State
20. _ _ _ _ _ _ _ Ø	dnaalyrm	Old Line State

The four states found in the circled letters are _____, _____, _____, and _____.

83. U.S. PRESIDENTS

❦

Code Name Cody has a unique way of remembering the U.S. Presidents. He uses what he calls "code names" for their last names. For instance Washington is "cleaning two thousand pounds." Be prepared to let your mind expand since Cody's clues force you to think hard about these names. Identify as many of these presidents by writing their names in the appropriate spaces.

Adams   Filmore   Harrison   Reagan
Bush   Ford   Hayes   Truman
Carter   Garfield   Kennedy   Tyler
Cleveland   Grant   Pierce   Wilson
Coolidge   Harding   Polk

1. _____ comic strip cat

2. _____ jab with a stick

3. _____ several male Garden of Eden residents

4. _____ an honest homo sapien

5. _____ allow

6. _____ confusion of the mind

7. _____ occupy additionally or pile higher

8. _____ one who hauls

9. _____ a woody plant

10. _____ a straight line weapon

11. _____ one who works with glazed, fired clay

12. _____ moderately cold rim

13. _____ stab

14. _____ hirsute male offspring

15. _____ a stream's shallow place

16. _____ becoming firmer

17. _____ William's male child

18. _____ to split the earth

19. _____ diminutives of Kenneth and Edward

Bonus: Name five different last names of U.S. Presidents that end with the letters "-son."

84. A CAPITAL TRIP

Are you ready to see the capital cities of the United States? Here is your opportunity! The catch is that only ten of these trips are possible since you can enter only a state that touches the one before it. Thus, you cannot go from Albany to Dover since their states are not next to one another. Write a letter Y if the trip can be made, and an N if it cannot.

1. ___ Albany—Harrisburg—Columbus—Oklahoma City

2. ___ Cheyenne—Pierre—Des Moines—Lincoln

3. ___ Bismarck—Helena—Boise—Salem

4. ___ Lansing—Indianapolis—Columbus—Harrisburg

5. ___ Hartford—Boston—Concord—Augusta

6. ___ Montgomery—Jackson—Little Rock—Springfield

7. ___ Annapolis—Dover—Trenton—Albany

8. ___ Sacramento—Carson City—Phoenix—Austin

9. ___ Madison—St. Paul—Bismarck—Denver

10. ___ Frankfort—Charleston—Harrisburg—Dover

11. ___ Nashville—Frankfort—Indianapolis—Lansing

12. ___ Augusta—Concord—Montpelier—Boston

13. ___ Raleigh—Juneau—Boise—Honolulu

14. ___ Harrisburg—Trenton—Albany—Hartford

15. ___ Tallahassee—Atlanta—Nashville—Santa Fe

85. WHERE AM I?

&c&

Here are twenty-three famous American cities. Based on the clues, write the correct American city in the space provided.

Annapolis   Honolulu   New Orleans   Saint Augustine
Boston   Indianapolis   New York City   Santa Fe
Chicago   Los Angeles   Oklahoma City   Washington, DC
Colorado Springs Milwaukee   Philadelphia
Gettysburg   Montgomery   Raleigh

1. _____ the "loop," O'Hare Airport, Field Museum

2. _____ Broad Street, Fairmount Park, Independence Hall, Congress Hall

3. _____ Motor Speedway, Indiana's Capital city

4. _____ New Mexico's capital city, the Palace

5. _____ United States National Cemetery, site of Abraham Lincoln's famous speech

6. _____ Alabama's capital city, Confederate White House

7. _____ Lake Michigan, Mitchell, Washington and Gordon Parks, Marquette University

8. _____ Beacon Hill, Fenway Park, Bunker Hill

9. _____ United States Naval Academy

10. _____ Potomac River, The White House, Washington Monument

11. _____ Empire State Building, Statue of Liberty, Central Park

12. _____ North Carolina's state capital, North Carolina State University

13. _____ oldest city in the United States

14. _____ Dodger Stadium, Hollywood and Vine, Hollywood Bowl

15. _____ Tulane University, Bourbon Street, Birthplace of jazz

16. _____ Cowboy Hall of Fame Museum

17. _____ Hawaii's capital city, pineapple canneries

18. _____ Pike's Peak, United States Air Force Academy

86. RHYMING WITH HISTORICAL FIGURES

Question: "What are the famous Greek philospher's containers?" Answer: "Aristotle's bottles." Using rhyming words, identify these other historical situations. The historical figures are in alphabetical order by their last names. Write your response in the appropriate space.

1. _____ The Green Mountain Boys' Ethan's four quarts

2. _____ Women's Rights leader Amelia's gossips

3. _____ French President Charles' shopping areas

4. _____ Austrian psychoanalyst Sigmund's empty spaces

5. _____ *The Star-Spangled Banner's* composer's waters

6. _____ Civil Rights' leader Martin's circles

7. _____ Portuguese explorer Ferdinand's fruits

8. _____ U.S. educator Horace's cookware

9. _____ U.S. painter Grandma's flowers

10. _____ U.S. music composer Cole's mandates

11. _____ U.S. humorist Will's avoiders

12. _____ U.S. physician Jonas' discussions

13. _____ U.S. psychologist B.F.'s diet pills

14. _____ *Uncle Tom's Cabin's* author's ills

15. _____ English architect Sir Christopher's writing implements

16. _____ U.S. religious leader Brigham's breathing organs

Name _____ Date _____ Period _____

87. THE IN CROWD

Each of the words listed below belongs to one of the groups in 1–13. Write the word in its correct space. By sequentially using the first letters of each correct answer, you will have the answer to the question, "What did the man do who completely settled his debts?" Write that answer after the last group.

apropos   *dupe*   *interlude*   *loyal*   *threaten*
artless   *envelop*   *league*   *quake*   *unequivocal*
defeat   *inaugurate*   *link*

1. _____ alliance   confederation   coalition   union

2. _____ begin   commence   start   initiate

3. _____ tremble   oscillate   vibrate   stagger

4. _____ clear   unmistakable   definite   absolute

5. _____ recess   pause   interruption   respite

6. _____ fool   pawn   gull   tool

7. _____ timely   aptly   pertinently   seasonably

8. _____ endanger   terrify   imperil   jeopardize

9. _____ sheathe   cover   encompass   case

10. _____ overwhelm   rout   subdue   crush

11. _____ genuine   sincere   candid   open

12. _____ connect   knot   couple   bridge

13. _____ faithful   patriotic   dedicated   devoted

The man who completely settled his debts _ _ _ _ _ _ _ _ _ _ _ _ _.

88. YOU ARE A PART OF ME

⤙⤙⤚⤚

In this exercise you are given a group's parts and are asked to identify the group's name. For example, if the parts you were given are Rhode Island, Massachusetts, Vermont, Maine, Connecticut, and New Hampshire, the group's name is the New England States.

GROUP'S NAME **PARTS**

1. _____ inside address   salutation   body   signature

2. _____ stalagmites   stalactites   crystal pool   helictites

3. _____ stamen   pistil   petal   bud

4. _____ Green Room   East Room   Lincoln Suite   State Dining Room

5. _____ warning track   coach's box   batter's box   pitcher's mound

6. _____ Federal Reserve Bank number   serial number   Treasury seal   portrait

7. _____ yarmulke   tallith   sepher   zizith

8. _____ muffler   radiator   transmission   battery

9. _____ sidebar   bench   plaintiff's table   witness stand

10. _____ masthead   taffrail   keel   companionway

11. _____ neck   root   dentin   enamel

12. _____ damper   flue collar   ash lip   combustion chamber

13. _____ copyright   byline   dateline   caption

14. _____ ladder   horn   bell   bucket

15. _____ center ring   spotlight   animal cage   trapeze

Compose five groups and exchange them with your classmates.

89. THE ODD-MAN OUT

It's not pleasant being the "odd-man out." Each of these fifteen groups contains a member that does not belong with the other four. Circle the one that does not belong, and then write the group's name in the blank next to the number. When you have correctly identified the fifteen "odd-men out," the first letters will form the name of a person who never wanted to be the "odd-man out." Write his name below the fifteenth group.

1. _____ julep   mead   lemonade   elegiac   cider

2. _____ Behan   Rawlings   Yeats   Synge   O'Casey

3. _____ cookie   torte   nectarine   brownie   tart

4. _____ link   merge   combine   graft   elegant

5. _____ marimba   kazoo   shaft   bassoon   clarinet

6. _____ rex   tatoo   tsar   swami   lion

7. _____ halcyon   error   fallacy   blunder   booboo

8. _____ philippic   diatribe   tirade   eulogy   harangue

9. _____ scullery   cellar   gallery   parlor   myopic

10. _____ Sydney Carton   Madame Defarge   Charles Darney   Iago   Jerry Cruncher

11. _____ provolone   nebulous   cheddar   feta   ricotta

12. _____ zoology   geology   botany   gastric   phonics

13. _____ blazer   jersey   cardigan   wicker   sweater

14. _____ ascot   bonnet   beanie   beret   coxcomb

15. _____ yelp   halibut   salmon   sardine   pickerel

The hidden name is _ _ _ _ _ _   _ _ _ _ _ _ _ _ _.

90. WHAT DO WE HAVE IN COMMON?

The items in each of these fifteen groups share something in common. Write what they have in common in the space provided. The first one is done for you.

1. _____ Verranzano-Narrows, Golden Gate, Mackinaw, London

2. _____ *Ebony, Sports Illustrated, Time, YM*

3. _____ Athos, Porthos, Aramis

4. _____ lira, franc, dinar, peso

5. _____ *Blubber, Superfudge, Tales of a Fourth Grade Nothing, Deenie*

6. _____ Raleigh, Balboa, Magellan, Drake

7. _____ Korean, Spanish-American, Civil, Revolutionary

8. _____ *The King and I, Carousel, Man of La Mancha, Pygmalion*

9. _____ Hog Butcher for the World, The Windy City, City of the Big Shoulders, Home of the Bears and Cubs

10. _____ Cod, Hatteras, Canaveral, Good Hope

11 _____ Right, Isoceles, Equilateral, Scalene

12. _____ McKinley, Rushmore, Whitney, Vesuvius

13. _____ Tallahassee, Albany, Phoenix, Sacramento

14. _____ bloomers, chauvinism, pasteurize, nicotine

15. _____ guru, rajah, swami, pariah

91. FOLLOW THE LETTER WORD GRID

Thirteen words that match the definitions below are hidden in this word grid. Each of the words has two letters that follow one another in the alphabet. In the word *refer*, f follows e in the alphabet as well as in the word.

Find the words in the grid and then write them next to their correct definitions. You'll know if your answers are correct since the words are listed alphabetically next to their correct definitions.

L	D	B	Y	W	D	O	E	N	M	O	E	T	U	L	V	W	K	Y
I	X	J	I	X	M	B	P	J	R	Q	D	S	L	I	A	T	E	D
H	Y	C	Z	L	A	T	F	U	V	A	I	P	W	S	R	P	X	J
K	L	E	A	V	S	D	C	R	M	B	R	A	F	T	O	Z	X	D
P	O	B	F	B	G	V	H	N	K	I	T	N	O	G	W	E	Y	E
H	P	Q	G	U	S	I	J	Q	L	M	S	N	U	V	D	T	U	K
E	H	C	A	M	T	E	S	U	Y	N	H	X	T	W	S	G	V	A
F	O	R	L	G	H	P	N	A	R	D	N	U	T	N	H	I	R	J
F	N	Y	J	A	U	X	Q	T	S	L	L	M	S	O	Q	E	F	C
I	E	B	F	C	W	P	R	X	C	K	Z	Y	O	Q	P	R	B	L
G	X	Z	C	K	O	I	H	G	B	F	T	D	H	O	P	E	D	M
Y	C	I	N	E	N	O	V	I	C	E	B	C	G	D	F	T	A	G
D	H	Q	B	A	P	I	M	A	J	K	T	L	S	H	R	Z	O	F
E	R	Z	M	X	S	W	Z	U	V	E	K	I	D	N	O	L	K	N

The definitions of the thirteen hidden words which are listed alphabetically below are:

a. _____ not present

b. _____ item

c. _____ a portrait or statue showing the likeness of a person

d. _____ the disembodied spirit of a dead person

e. _____ gulping sound

f. _____ site of the 1898 Yukon Territory gold rush

g. _____ salve

h. _____ condemn

i. _____ beginner

j. _____ musical drama

k. _____ a long step

l. _____ treeless plain

m. _____ musical instrument with bars of various lengths

92. WORDS WITH THE SUFFIX -OLOGY

Here are twenty-five words that end with the -ology (a branch of learning) combination of letters. Fill in the missing letters of the defined words all dealing with learning or the study of a subject. Then identify the three names in the circles followed by the field with which they are associated.

1. physical nature of the earth _ O _ _ _ _ _
2. society and human relations _ _ _ O _ _ _ _ _
3. the nervous system O _ _ _ _ _ _ _ _
4. beauty culture _ _ O _ _ _ _ _ _ _ _
5. the nature of diseases _ _ O _ _ _ _ _ _
6. God and religious doctrine _ _ O _ _ _ _ _
7. animal and plant life _ O _ _ _ _ _
8. zoology dealing with insects _ O _ _ _ _ _ _ _ _
9. living organisms and their environment _ O _ _ _ _ _
10. music _ O _ _ _ _ _ _ _
11. rocks _ _ _ O _ _ _ _ _
12. poisons _ _ _ O _ _ _ _ _ _
13. atmosphere and weather _ _ _ O _ _ _ _ _ _ _
14. foretelling the future via the stars _ _ _ _ _ _ _ O _
15. the skin and its diseases _ _ _ _ O _ _ _ _ _ _
16. animals _ _ _ O _ _ _
17. industrial arts _ O _ _ _ _ _ _ _ _
18. animal fossils _ _ _ _ _ O _ _ _ _ _ _
19. the mind _ O _ _ _ _ _ _ _
20. life and cultures of the ancients _ _ O _ _ _ _ _ _ _
21. functions and processes of living organisms _ _ _ _ O _ _ _ _ _
22. origin and development of words O _ _ _ _ _ _ _ _
23. humans and cultural characteristics _ O _ _ _ _ _ _ _ _ _ _
24. drugs _ _ _ _ _ _ O _ _ _ _ _
25. human muscular movements _ _ _ O _ _ _ _ _ _ _

The three names found in the circles are _____, _____, and _____. Their field of study was _____.

Section IV

The Land of Literature

93. DO YOU HAVE THE MIDAS TOUCH?

If you have the "Midas touch," everything you touch turns to gold. Literally, things turn out pretty well for you. Below are names of memorable literary characters. Match these names with what they mean to us today. Perhaps you will prove that you have the Midas touch!

1. ___ SCROOGE

2. ___ TARZAN

3. ___ ROMEO

4. ___ LILLIPUTIANS

5. ___ MALAPROP

6 ___ YAHOOS

7. ___ BIG BROTHER

8. ___ POLLYANNA

9. ___ SHYLOCK

10. ___ SHERLOCK

11. ___ UGLY DUCKLING

12. ___ HECTOR

13. ___ MENTOR

14. ___ FRIDAY

15. ___ MIDAS

16. ___ JEKYLL AND HYDE

A. reliable person

B. exacting creditor

C. magic touch

D. tutor

E. wise crime solver

F. miser

G. the eternal optimist

H. crude people

I. one who in time becomes beautiful or important

J. misusing words

K. to bully

L. lover

M. one who changes from one condition to another

N. one who invades privacy and likes to control

O. strongman

P. small people

Bonus: Write down five more literary characters and what their names mean to us today.

94. AMERICAN WRITERS' WORD FIND

Thirty–four American authors are hidden in this puzzle. The names are written forward, backwards, diagonally, up and down. Upon completing the puzzle, select one author and research what kind of novels, poems, or stories he or she wrote. Discuss your findings with your classmates.

```
G N O S N I K C I D F D Z F W T X
Y Z J N H R R N X W Z M C J H W J
K O W G E A R R O P H L T O K K K
L E N T N H E E T D O I R W F R Z
P S R E T S A M B E N E T R A H X
B O T O I Z A W C R A O O M T I G
P N N E U L Y L T U U S L A A W N
M B R I I A L U I H T H L F I N K
Q D V O L N C E P N O P T L Z H D
X K S L B K B M M D G R D D S N M
K C I A I N E E E I E N K X R R
X M J V N R N A C L R K R E E Z S
K P V N Z D V S R K V S E P R C M
W K S W C Z B I O F W I O C H F Q
J A C K S O N U N N F O L N Q F X
C U M M I N G S R G C K G L G H K
H E M I N G W A Y G C A T H E R R
```

BENET	FRANKLIN	LONDON	ROBINSON
CATHER	FROST	MASTERS	SALINGER
COOPER	HARTE	MELVILLE	SANDBURG
CRANE	HAWTHORNE	MILLAY	STEINBECK
CUMMINGS	HEMINGWAY	O'NEIL	THOREAU
DICKINSON	IRVING	PLATH	THURBER
DREISER	JACKSON	POE	TWAIN
EMERSON	KEROUAC	PORTER	UPDIKE
			WHITMAN
			WILDER

95. ONOMATO WHAT???

One of the more memorable terms of literature is "onomatopoeia". That word and nineteen other literary terms are included in this crossword puzzle featuring terms from the field of literature. The list of choices is offered beneath the clues.

ACROSS CLUES

3. story that has a hidden or symbolic meaning
5. a fourteen line poem
7. nonsense poem in five lines
10. story written in dialogue form for actors on stage
11. a dramatic speech intended to be heard only by the speaker and the audience
15. a section of a novel
18. a section of a poem
19. agreement in sound between two syllables
20. the story's main character

DOWN CLUES

1. style using sarcasm and wit
2. a poem that tells a story in short stanzas
4. a long, narrative poem about a hero
6. a medium-length poem in praise of a person or thing
8. poem mourning the death of a person
9. two consecutive rhyming lines of poetry
12. a word that imitates the sound of the action ("hiss" is an example)
13. metrical foot of one short syllable followed by a long syllable
14. story having a moral and animals as characters
16. short composition dealing with a specific topic
17. shorter than a soliloquy, words spoken by the actor intended to be heard by the audience only

WORD LIST

ALLEGORY	COUPLET	ESSAY	ODE	SATIRE
ASIDE	DRAMA	FABLE	ONOMATOPOEIA	SOLILOQUY
BALLAD	ELEGY	IAMBIC	PROTAGONIST	SONNET
CHAPTER	EPIC	LIMERICK	RHYME	STANZA

96. SWISH, BOOM, BAM!

Swish, boom, bam...words whose sounds tell us a lot about themselves. They are examples of the poetic term, *onomatopoeia*. Words whose sounds suggest their meanings are onomatopoeic. To form onomatopoeic words, connect letters in the adjacent boxes below. You may use the same letter twice in a row or as often as needed to help form a word. Find ten words in the grid below, and you're good; find sixteen or more, and you're a champion!

P	W	S	P	H
C	O	K	I	A
L	M	O	Z	E
A	W	N	B	U
N	G	K	A	Y

Now try to describe the sound of each of the words you formed.

© 1994 by the Center for Applied Research in Education

Name _____ Date _____ Period _____

97. DON'T READ THESE BOOKS!

Twenty–two books that were censored, objected to or banned at one time are the clues to this crossword puzzle. Fill in the books' authors. Later you might discuss with your teacher and classmates why these books were banned.

ACROSS CLUES

1. Ulysses
5. To Kill a Mockingbird
6. Huckleberry Finn
8. Brave New World
9. Lady Chatterley's Lover
10. Doctor Zhivago
12. The Dead Zone
13. Catch–22
16. Uncle Tom's Cabin
17. A Farewell to Arms
19. Soul on Ice
20. The Naked and the Dead
21. Another Country

DOWN CLUES

2. Tobacco Road
3. Catcher in the Rye
4. Slaughterhouse Five
7. The Color Purple
11. Of Mice and Men
14. Elmer Gantry
15. The Merchant of Venice
18. Invisible Man
20. Tropic of Cancer

WORD LIST

BALDWIN	HEMINGWAY	LEE	SALINGER	VONNEGUT
CALDWELL	HUXLEY	LEWIS	SHAKESPEARE	WALKER
CLEAVER	JOYCE	MAILER	STEINBECK	
ELLISON	KING	MILLER	STOWE	
HELLER	LAWRENCE	PASTERNAK	TWAIN	

107

98. OBJECTION! I WANT THAT BOOK BANNED RIGHT NOW!!

These thirteen titles are books that were either banned, objected to, or censored for any number of reasons. Fill in these titles and then discuss with your classmates possible reasons why these titles, or other pieces of literature, might be banned or censored. How many other books do you know that have been questioned? An interesting dilemma. . . .

ACROSS CLUES

1. John Updike
5. John Steinbeck
6. Anne Tyler
8. William Faulkner
11. Pearl Buck
12. Margaret Mitchell
13. Edna Ferber

DOWN CLUES

2. Marjorie Kinnan Rawlings
3. Saul Bellow
4. Bernard Malamud
7. Sinclair Lewis
9. William Faulkner
10. Toni Morrison

WORD LIST

A FABLE
ARROWSMITH
BELOVED
BREATHING LESSONS
GONE WITH THE WIND

HUMBOLDTS GIFT
RABBIT IS RICH
SO BIG
THE GRAPES OF WRATH

THE GOOD EARTH
THE YEARLING
THE FIXER
THE REIVERS

99. THE FOOD OF LITERATURE

Literature...food for thought. How many of these titles containing food can you identify? Do you know who wrote them? First write the correct food in the space and then match the title with its author. One author is used twice. The first one is done for you.

TITLE

1. _E_ A Raisin in the Sun
2. ___ The _____ of Wrath
3. ___ After _____ Picking
4. ___ A Clockwork _____
5. ___ The _____ Orchard
6. ___ The _____ War
7. ___ The Princess and the _____
8. ___ Super _____
9. ___ Rumble _____
10. ___ The Wild _____
11. ___ _____ and Ale
12. ___ The Tale of Peter _____
13. ___ _____ Flat
14. ___ _____, Run
15. ___ The Enormous _____
16. ___ Green _____ and _____
17. ___ The Velveteen _____
18. ___ The _____ slayer
19. ___ The Snow _____
20. ___ The Catcher in the _____

AUTHOR

A. James Fenimore Cooper
B. Judy Blume
C. J.D. Salinger
D. Paul Gallico
E. Lorraine Hansberry
F. John Steinbeck
G. Margary Williams
H. S.E. Hinton
I. Dr. Seuss
J. Anton Chekhov
K. Robert Frost
L. Anthony Burgess
M. Oliver Butterworth
N. John Updike
O. Robert Cormier
P. Hans Christian Andersen
Q. W.S. Maugham
R. Henrik Ibsen
S. Beatrix Potter
T. John Steinbeck

How many examples of song, movie, or television program titles can you remember that have food in them? Work as a class to write down as many as possible.

100. FORMS OF LITERATURE

The names of fifteen forms of literature are scrambled up below. Unscramble them and write their correctly spelled names on the lines next to the numbers.

1. _____ ciep

2. _____ riday

3. _____ hepsec

4. _____ nelged

5. _____ seays

6. _____ ayfir teal

7. _____ fklo elat

8. _____ oraunlj

9. _____ borigahyp

10. _____ atuborigayhop

11. _____ levno

12. _____ ylpa

13. _____ pmeo

14. _____ hrtso sryto

15. _____ eshist

Name _____ Date _____ Period _____

101. THE TERMS OF THEATRICAL PRODUCTIONS

Twenty terms associated with the theater are the answers to this crossword puzzle. These terms have been used by the theatrical world for thousands of years. The ancient Greek playwrights, Aeschylus, Sophocles, and Euripedes used these terms just as modern day dramatists do today. Fill in the correct answers in their appropriate spaces.

ACROSS CLUES

2. the high point and usually most exciting part of the play
5. a literary composition that includes dialogue and actors
6. words spoken by an actor intended for only the audience and not the other actors to hear
11. two sides in opposition
12. talk between actors
14. set of clothes worn by the actors
15. the main character in the play
17. the part of the play that explains the plot
18. a division in the play; Shakespeare generally had five in his plays

DOWN CLUES

1. the principal role in the play
3. group of people watching the play
4. a play that usually has a disastrous ending for one or more of the characters
7. backdrops, props and such designed for scenes in a play
8. practicing a play
9. a play division within an act
10. one who controls a play by instructing the actors
13. a long speech by one actor
14. a turning point in the play
15. the author of the play
16. arrangement of incidents in a play

WORD LIST

ACT	COSTUMES	LEAD	REHEARSAL
ASIDE	CRISIS	MONOLOGUE	RESOLUTION
AUDIENCE	DIALOGUE	PLAYWRIGHT	SCENE
CLIMAX	DIRECTOR	PLOT	SET
CONFLICT	DRAMA	PROTAGONIST	TRAGEDY

102. LITERARY RHYME TIME

Have some rhyming fun with authors. Shakespeare's properties are the *bard's yards*, and Salinger's female friends are *J.D.'s ladies*. Put you brains and ears together and fill in these blanks with rhyming words.

1. _____ _____ Melville's friends from Munich

2. _____ _____ Whitman's seasonings

3. _____ _____ *The Last of the Mohicans'* author's spies

4. _____ _____ A zealous Mr. Hemingway

5. _____ _____ A blunt Mr. Vonnegut

6. _____ _____ Poetess Sylvia's ires

7. _____ _____ Willy Loman's creator's plant's shoots

8. _____ _____ Poet Langston's opinions

9. _____ _____ Poet William Butler's partners

10. _____ _____ Poet Ezra's heaps of dirt

11. _____ _____ A missing "The Road Not Taken's" creator

12. _____ _____ Novelist Austen's hurting sensation

13. _____ _____ Blind Greek epic poet's nomads

14. _____ _____ Author Morrison's young horses

15. _____ _____ Playwright Hansberry's tracts of ground

16. _____ _____ "The Rape of the Lock's" author's cords

17. _____ _____ "Songs of Innocence" author's desserts

18. _____ _____ "Ode to a Nightingale's" author's places to sit

19. _____ _____ *Frankenstein's* author's toast spreads

20. _____ _____ *Dubliners* author's options

103. THE TOOLS OF POETRY

Poetry, like any of the literary genres, has the ability to move us. Much of poetry's success is due to the poetic devices that the poet employs throughout the poem. Identify the twenty poetic terms described below. Then you might try composing your own poetic lines that use these terms.

ACROSS CLUES

3. a figure of speech in which something very closely associated with a thing stands for it
4. an elaborate phrase that describes persons, things or events in an indirect way
5. the repetition of sounds in two or more words or phrases that appear close to each other
9. a section or division of a long poem
10. the repetition of initial consonant sounds
12. verse written in unrhymed iambic pentameter
15. two consecutive lines of poetry that rhyme
16. a figure of speech that combines opposite or contradictory ideas or terms
17. a long narrative poem telling the deeds of a culture's hero and the values of that culture
18. a fourteen line poem, usually written in rhymed iambic pentameter

DOWN CLUES

1. a figure of speech using exaggeration, or overstatement, for special effect
2. a stanza or poem of four lines
6. a kind of metaphor that makes a comparison between two startlingly different things
7. a poem of mourning, usually over the death of an individual
8. a story told in verse and usually meant to be sung
9. a break or pause in a line of poetry
10. a figure of speech in which an absent or dead person, or an abstract quality, is addressed
11. a figure of speech that makes a comparison between two things that are basically dissimilar
13. a complex, lengthy poem written in dignified style about a serious subject
14. a comparison made between two things through the use of a specific word of comparison

WORD LIST

ALLITERATION	CAESURA	ELEGY	METAPHOR	QUATRAIN
APOSTROPHE	CANTO	EPIC	METONYMY	RHYTHM
BALLAD	CONCEIT	HYPERBOLE	ODE	SIMILE
BLANK VERSE	COUPLET	KENNING	OXYMORON	SONNET

104. UNSCRAMBLING POETIC TERMS

Twenty-four poetic terms are just waiting for you to unscramble them. The first letter in the scrambled version of the terms is also the first letter in the real spelling of the term. Write your answers in the spaces next to the words.

1. AETCNC _____

2. AYERLOGL _____

3. AUSNLOIL _____

4. AAENPTS _____

5. AOPEHTPOSR _____

6. ASSAECNNO _____

7. BDALLA _____

8. BAKLN VRESE _____

9. CAYCHNOPO _____

10. CASERUA _____

11. CETOLPU _____

12. DTLCYA _____

13. EPNOUYH _____

14. FOTO _____

15. HUAKI _____

16. IABM _____

17. IRYNO _____

18. LMIKECIR _____

19. MTERAOHP _____

20. METYYNMO _____

21. PRAAXOD _____

22. QARUTIAN _____

23. RHTYMH _____

24. SACINNSO _____

105. MORE POETIC TERMS

Here are some more poetic terms that will help you to gain a greater appreciation for poetry. Practice writing examples of these terms.

ACROSS CLUES

1. five lines of anapestic meter usually used for a humorous or nonsensical purpose
5. a harsh, unpleasant sounding choice and arrangement of sounds within a line of poetry
8. the dictionary definition of a word
9. a repeated word, phrase, line or group of lines at a fixed position within a poem
10. the stress that a syllable is given
11. a three-line poem, from Japan, that has lines of 5, 7, and 5 syllables respectively
12. an historical or literary reference used explicitly or implicitly
13. the poet's attitude toward his subject
14. pleasant sounding choice of words
18. a sonnet consisting of an octave and a sestet with a rhyme scheme such as abbaabbacdcdcd
19. the use of a word that imitates its meaning in sound (crunch is an example)

DOWN CLUES

2. what a word suggests beyond its dictionary definition (naive as an example)
3. also called the Shakespearean sonnet; it consists of 14 lines whose rhyme is ababcdcdefefgg
4. language intended to indicate an incongruity between two things, situations or people
6. a poem about dawn
7. verse that has no set meter
10. a narrative or a description intended to tell a story and/or teach a lesson
15. an apparently contradictory circumstance or statement
16. ridicule, usually exaggerated, whose intention is to make the reader laugh and think
17. the major idea of a poem

WORD LIST

ACCENT	CACOPHONY	EUPHONY	ITALIAN SONNET	REFRAIN
ALLEGORY	CONNOTATION	FREE VERSE	LIMERICK	SATIRE
ALLUSION	DENOTATION	HAIKU	ONOMATOPOEIA	THEME
AUBADE	ENGLISH SONNET	IRONY	PARADOX	TONE

106. THE POETS' PLACE

෨ᕲᏋᕲᓈ

Three quotes by famous poets are hidden in this cryptogram. The poet's name is below the quote. Solve the cryptogram by substituting the correct letters for the letters used in the code. No letter can stand for itself. Set up the substitution code at the bottom of the page. Good luck.

1. PXU NXRFF NIG R FDTDG GU GXI DAKFWIAYI UK R XWTRA

EIDAM?

VRFSX PRFZU ITIVNUA

2. IZWYRGDUA DN GXI REDFDGJ GU FDNGIA GU RFTUNG

RAJGXDAM PDGXUWG FUNDAM JUWV GITSIV UV JUWV

NIFK–YUAKDZIAYI.

VUEIVG KVUNG

3. R SUIG DN, EIKUVI RAJGXDAM IFNI, R SIVNUA PXU DN

SRNNDUARGIFJ DA FUOI PDGX FRAMWRMI.

P.X. RWZIA

Real letters: A B C D E F G H I J K L M N O P Q R S T U V W X Y Z

Substitute
letters: –

107. POPULAR MAGAZINES

There are seventeen magazines in this word find. After you have located them all, research what type of articles each of them carries. Discuss the results with your classmates.

```
J V S K M K Q V N Y V K P W S P R K N C G T J Y
B X B C B A R R N R M C P R V K K V V R V V D K
M R G Y I Y E O X S E H Q A T V X D B K Y G J Y
F M G P R N P R A L Z D V Z R Q Q H Y J F H W V
C J M C B K A J T D U Z B L V E W G W X B P S X
K X C Y S Z H H R S A F S O Q R N H P E G H T H
V C R T Y D Z X C S D N I D O H W T S Z M J D T
C F L S E V E N T E E N D T G K V E S Q U I R E
T R Z Y M Q W F Q R M H A T U V E E H U L O T H
Q X X R N Z C Y L O S R M D R A M B Q R P S G X
T Y M D X T M T T X V B A F L A E W O S W G G K
R K V W X F K D F J D X C L G E C B B N R H Q Q
T R V Z N T Z C Y W H Z T G U S I K E C Y J Y Z
N K K Q T R F M B J L Y R M L P B F H S S T B P
R E A D E R S D I G E S T W K J O P W H U H J Y
Q L B D J L V V H R L D G T L R P P M G H O F K
S P O R T S I L L U S T R A T E D J Z F Q Y H Q
```

EBONY
ESQUIRE
FIELD AND STREAM
GAMES
HOUSE BEAUTIFUL
OMNI

PARENTS
POPULAR MECHANICS
READERS DIGEST
REDBOOK
ROAD AND TRACK
SEVENTEEN

SPORT
SPORTS ILLUSTRATED
TIME
US
YM

108. LITERARY TITLES IN FRENCH

Had Harriet Beecher Stowe written her novel, *Uncle Tom's Cabin* in France, she would have entitled it *La Case de l'oncle Tom*. Match the French with their English titles.

1. ___ The Age of Innocence
2. ___ Alice's Adventures in Wonderland
3. ___ All Quiet on the Western Front
4. ___ Arms and the Man
5. ___ The Black Arrow
6. ___ The Cherry Orchard
7. ___ Crime and Punishment
8. ___ For Whom the Bell Tolls
9. ___ Gone with the Wind
10. ___ The Grapes of Wrath
11. ___ Great Expectations
12. ___ A Handful of Dust
13. ___ The Hunchback of Notre Dame
14. ___ The Importance of Being Earnest
15. ___ The Last of the Mohicans
16. ___ The Little Prince
17. ___ Long Day's Journey into Night
18. ___ A Midsummer Night's Dream
19. ___ Pride and Prejudice
20. ___ A Streetcar Named Desire

a. Autant en emporte le vent
b. Notre Dame de Paris
c. Pour qui sonne le glas
d. Orgveil et Préjugés
e. Le héros et le soldat
f. Alice au pays des merveilles
g. A la ouest rien de nouveau
h. Crime et châtiment
i. Le songe d'une nuit d'été
j. Long voyage dans la nuit
k. le Petit Prince
l. Les raisins de la colère
m. La Flêche noire
n. L'âge d'innocence
o. La cerisaie
p. Un tramway nommé Desir
q. Une poignée de poussière
r. De l'importance d'être constant
s. Les grandes Espérances
t. Le dernier des Mohicans

109. BIBLICALLY SPEAKING

How familiar are you with the names of people found in the Bible? Here are twenty Biblical characters and a brief description of each. Fill in the correct names from the list below.

ACROSS CLUES

1. builder of the first temple; king of Israel
5. raised from the dead by Jesus
6. killed by David
10. Abel's brother
11. associated with lying; a high priest
12. Jerusalem's destroyer
16. associated with the word "doubting"
17. father of Jesus
19. mother of Jesus
20. washed Jesus' feet and witnessed his resurrection

DOWN CLUES

2. his wife was turned into a pillar of salt
3. betrayed Jesus for 30 pieces of silver
4. associated with the word "patience"
7. nearly sacrificed by Abraham
8. was given the Ten Commandments
9. Abraham's wife
13. one of the Three Wise Men
14. mandated the death of children
15. tried and condemned Jesus Christ
18. originally named Saul

WORD LIST

ANANIAS	JOSEPH	NEBUCHADNEZZAR
BALTHAZAR	JUDAS ISCARIOT	PAUL
CAIN	LAZARUS	PONTIUS PILATE
GOLIATH	LOT	SARAH
HEROD	MARY	SOLOMON
ISAAC	MARY MAGDALENE	THOMAS
JOB	MOSES	

110. QUOTABLE QUOTES

The words that make up ten famous quotes are jumbled up below. Write the words in their correct order and then match the person who is quoted by writing the correct letter in the appropriate space next to the quote.

a. Elizabeth Barrett Browning
b. Robert Burns
c. Charles Dickens
d. John Donne
e. Benjamin Franklin

f. Robert Frost
g. Robert Herrick
h. John Keats
i. Joyce Kilmer
j. Martin Luther King, Jr.

1. ___ man an island no is.

   _____

2. ___ dream I a have.

   _____

3. ___ good good neighbors fences make.

   _____

4. ___ a beauty forever of joy thing a is.

   _____

5. ___ my red a red like rose o Luve's.

   _____

6. ___ penny is earned a saved a penny.

   _____

7. ___ ye may while rosebuds ye gather.

   _____

8. ___ it the times, times of was was it the of worst best.

   _____

9. ___ do I how thee love? me let ways count the.

   _____

10. ___ God made by tree poems me are like only a fools make but can.

    _____

111. ROYALTY IN LITERARY TITLES

Each of the twenty literary titles contains a title pertaining to royalty. The author of each work is given. The first one is done for you.

TITLE	AUTHOR
1. The <u>Count</u> of Monte Cristo	Alexander Dumas
2. The _____ and the Pauper	Mark Twain
3. The African _____	C.S. Forester
4. The _____ of the Rings	J.R.R. Tolkien
5. A Connecticut Yankee in _____ Arthur's Court	Mark Twain
6. The Little _____	Antoine de Saint-Exupéry
7. _____ Lear	William Shakespeare
8. _____ Henry VIII	William Shakespeare
9. _____ Jim	Joseph Conrad
10. The _____	Niccolo Machiavelli
11. All the _____ 's Men	Robert Penn Warren
12. The _____ Jones	Eugene O'Neill
13. Oedipus _____	Sophocles
14. The _____ and the Pea	Hans Christian Andersen
15. The _____ 's New Clothes	Hans Christian Andersen
16. The Little _____	Frances H. Burnett
17. My Last _____	Robert Browning
18. Little _____ Fauntleroy	Frances H. Burnett
19. _____ Rat	James Clavell
20. Ode on the Death of the _____ of Wellington	Alfred Lord Tennyson

112. SHAKESPEARE'S FAMOUS THIRTEEN

Thirteen of Shakespeare's plays are found in this crossword puzzle. With clues featuring settings, characters, or quotes, identify these well-known Shakespearean plays.

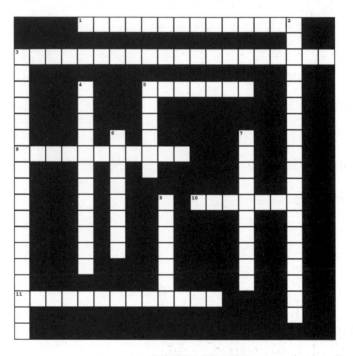

ACROSS CLUES

1. "A pair of star-cross'd lovers"
2. Helena, Bertram, King of France
5. Boar's Head Tavern, Prince Hal, Falstaff, Hotspur
8. The Forest of Arden, Oliver, Orlando, Rosalind
10. a Moor, Desdemona, Iago, a handkerchief
11. Alcibiades, a cave, a patron of the arts

DOWN CLUES

2. Antonio, Shylock, Portia, "a pound of flesh"
3. Roman civil war, an asp, Octavius, suicide due to a rumor
4. "Beware the ides of March," Cassius, Brutus, ". . . the most unkindest cut of all."
5. Ophelia, Polonius, Denmark, Gertrude, "Frailty, thy name is woman."
6. Goneril, Regan, and Cordelia; Gloucester, Edmund
7. Prospero, Miranda, Ariel, Caliban
9. "Fair is foul . . ."; three Witches, Banquo, sleepwalking scene

WORD LIST

ALL'S WELL THAT ENDS WELL
ANTONY AND CLEOPATRA
AS YOU LIKE IT
HAMLET
HENRY IV

JULIUS CAESAR
KING LEAR
MACBETH
OTHELLO

ROMEO AND JULIET
THE MERCHANT OF VENICE
THE TEMPEST
TIMON OF ATHENS

Section V

Making Language Work for You

A YY I CCCC CC NN

113. BET ON A TIE

This race between our three racers, sentence (S), fragment (F), and run-on (RO), will end in a tie. No kidding! Write the appropriate letter in each blank. If you've answered these questions correctly, each contestant will have gained the same number of lengths. Add up your lengths as shown by the number after each group of words and see the race end in a tie.

1. _____ Here is the first question. (2)

2. _____ Never before in the history of mankind. (3)

3. _____ Over the river and through the woods to grandmother's house. (2)

4. _____ Turn the light off, it's too bright in here. (4)

5. _____ Do you believe everything you hear? (1)

6. _____ This is the best movie, it's hilarious. (3)

7. _____ Mike and Frank are in charge here. (3)

8. _____ Help me I'm having trouble with this problem. (2)

9. _____ Whether or not you plan on going to the dance. (2)

10. _____ Today is the first day of the contest. (1)

11. _____ Jocelyn, the girl in the first row of Mr. Smith's class. (2)

12. _____ Mississippi is a state and a river. (1)

13. _____ If I can help, please let me know. (1)

Each of the three contestants gained _____ lengths.

114. AN EVEN DOZEN

This activity challenges you to distinguish between sentences, fragments, and run-ons. For each group of words that is a sentence, write S and the number 1 before the sentence. For each fragment, write F and the number 2. For each run–on, write RO and the number 3. When each set is totaled up, the value of each should be an even dozen. The first one is done for you.

SET 1

A. <u>RO</u>   <u>3</u>   Turn the light on, it's dark in here.

B. ____   ___   I like the scene from the shore.

C. ____   ___   Bringing home the money from the raffle.

D. ____   ___   Every once in a while he can be silly.

E. ____   ___   Knowing quite well that I was not happy with his behavior.

F. ____   ___   I know you can win the game, just try very hard.

SET 2

A. ____   ___   The man in the blue suit who is watching the game.

B. ____   ___   Kenny is the man to choose, he is the best candidate.

C. ____   ___   Maureen is my math tutor.

D. ____   ___   Not really seeing the car in front of us.

E. ____   ___   Kate, the new student, reading the library book here.

F. ____   ___   Over the river and through the woods in a hurry.

115. DIRECT ME TO YOUR OBJECT!

❧❧❧

A direct object is a noun or pronoun that receives the action of the verb. It answers the question "What?" or "Whom?"after the action verb. Circle the ten direct objects found in these sentences. Then beneath the last sentence write the activity with which all of these objects are associated.

1. We asked the guard for directions to the museum.

2. The photographer developed his shot of the accident.

3. Our principal asked the substitute for her class list.

4. The band director purchased uniforms for the marching band.

5. The young children can carry their baskets on the trip.

6. Yvonne cracked the rim of the coffee cup.

7. We learned some interesting stuff about reptiles yesterday.

8. The retired professor enjoyed the travel.

9. They could hear the swish of the cane swinging through the air.

10. The hunters set the net for the wild animal.

The direct objects are all associated with what activity? _____

116. THE PLANE FLEW _____ THE CLOUDS

Though not all prepositions can fit into the sentence above, many can. Not a bad way to remember many prepositions! Underline the thirteen prepositional phrases found in the sentences below. Using the first letters of the words in these phrases (in order), you will find the names of four boys and four girls.

1. Jonathan went to Harry's old mother to ask for help.

2. After Sunday I'll be able to help you more.

3. Yvonne bought a house near Arlington.

4. Near Connie's yacht is a beautiful park.

5. He left during intermission.

6. Jerry raced his canoe against nine Eskimos.

7. He read the novel by Rita's interesting American niece.

8. On Sunday he wrote a paper concerning Ayn Rand.

9. The painting by Eddie was given to Tom Young.

10. He went out for lunch.

11. On any routine Thursday I will do some reading and shopping.

The four boys' names are _____, _____, _____, and _____.

The four girls' names are _____, _____, _____, and _____.

© 1994 by the Center for Applied Research in Education

117. A SCORE OF ADVERBS FOR THE TAKING

Circle the twenty adverbs in these sentences. Then taking the first letter in each of the twenty adverbs (in order), write the name of a famous inventor and his invention below the last sentence.

1. He crudely grabbed the paper from her hands.

2. Yesterday you readily helped with the project.

3. Oliver usually does his work silently.

4. Regina meekly asked if he could casually mention the fact.

5. Cautiously I approached the closed door.

6. Molly openly admitted that Bob rashly hit the wall.

7. Ginny merely said that you acted inanely and cowardly.

8. She keenly pointed to the guilty man.

9. Rarely will you see a player exactly like Lyle.

10. Apparently the paper will precisely print the news item.

11. The players were distributed evenly.

12. The class members stood rigidly awaiting the results.

The inventor is _ _ _ _ _ _ _ _ _ _ _ _ _ _ and his invention is the _ _ _ _ _ _.

118. WEARING DIFFERENT HATS

❦

Several words are used as different parts of speech in these fifteen sentences. Write the part of speech of the underlined word in the appropriate space.

adjective   *conjunction*   *noun*   *pronoun*
adverb   *interjection*   *preposition*   *verb*

1. _____ We need to buy a *snow* shovel.

2. _____ Do you think it will *snow* tonight?

3. _____ *Snow* is beautiful.

4. _____ What are we having *for* dinner?

5. _____ I can't go out, *for* I have little spare time.

6. _____ Walk *down* the hall quietly.

7. _____ *Down* the ball.

8. _____ He fell *down* after he caught the ball.

9. _____ The *down* payment is usually reasonable.

10. _____ The duck's *down* was soft.

11. _____ *Light* the stove please.

12. _____ He lifted the *light* package.

13. _____ A *light* was visible from a distance.

14. _____ *Let* is a tennis term.

15. _____ I *let* him back into the room.

Find the eight different parts of speech in this sentence. Abbreviate the part of speech above each word.

Oh, I can barely go to the game since I have little money.

119. TWO BY TWO BY TWO BY TWO BY TWO . . .

Though the title may sound rather confusing, it does make sense, if you look at it in this way. Take the first two letters of each word that is the part of speech in the bracket before each sentence. If you do this sequentially for sentences one through ten, you will compose a familiar saying. Underline the word requested in each sentence and write the word's first two letters in the spaces provided after the last sentence. The first one is done for you.

1. (verb) The last train <u>left</u> at eleven o'clock.

2. (noun) Aviation is interesting for me.

3. (noun) We saw the ewe later on.

4. (adverb) The hall was decorated elegantly.

5. (proper noun) Leo is the star of the high school musical.

6. (pronoun) Nobody is denied the right to vote.

7. (adjective) She felt it was ugly to say the least.

8. (interjection) Ha! I knew that was his name.

9. (adverb) After the game Bob felt lower than his brother did.

10. (pronoun) Neither can do the problem easily.

<u>L</u> <u>e</u> _ _ _   _ _ _ _   _ _ _ _ _ _   _ _ _ _ _.

120. GRANDMA KNOWS GRAMMAR!

Grandma has a knack for grammatical terms. Match your wits against Grandma by correctly matching these terms with their definitions. Write your answers in the spaces provided.

___ 1. ADJECTIVE

___ 2. COMMON NOUN

___ 3. VERB

___ 4. GERUND

___ 5. PROPER NOUN

___ 6. PRONOUN

___ 7. PARTICIPLE

___ 8. CONTRACTION

___ 9. CONJUNCTION

___ 10. INFINITIVE

___ 11. ADVERB

___ 12. ARTICLE

___ 13. COMPOUND WORD

___ 14. PREPOSITION

___ 15. COLLECTIVE NOUN

___ 16. NOUN

A. connects words, phrases, clauses or sentences

B. a noun that refers to a group

C. noun that refers to a specific person or thing

D. modifies a verb, adjective, or adverb

E. the word *to* plus a verb

F. a word shortened by omission

G. name of a person, place, thing, or idea

H. a word that takes the place of a noun

I. an action word

J. *a, an,* or *the* indicating a noun

K. a name referring to one or a class

L. modifies a noun or a pronoun

M. two words used to form one larger word

N. a verb that acts as an adjective

O. word ending in -ing and acting as a noun

P. word that relates one word to an object

Bonus: What famous Grandma gained fame in the field of painting? _____

© 1994 by the Center for Applied Research in Education

121. THE VERB'S THE WORD

Underline the verb in each of these twelve sentences. Then using the first letter of each verb (in order), find the answer to the question, " When is a door not a door?" Write your answer in the spaces below the last sentence.

1. The man watered the flowers every morning.

2. Happiness has its many pleasures.

3. Eventually Eddie enlisted in the army.

4. Neither a borrower nor a lender needs additional advice.

5. A cat inched its way toward the mouse.

6. These creatures terrified the smaller rodent.

7. Many players intimidate their opponents before the game.

8. Our coach shuffled the players in and out of the game.

9. The humorous teacher added the numbers on the blackboard.

10. Joseph justified his actions to the committee members.

11. She answered the questions on the difficult examination.

12. Molly replied quite readily.

When is a door not a door? _ _ _ _ _ _ _ _ _ _ _ _!

122. HOW IRREGULAR!

Irregular verbs form their past and past participles in ways different from regular verbs. The verb *go* is an example of an irregular verb. Select the correct (past or past participle) of the given verb. Then, using the circled letters in order, identify a famous American personality.

1. drive   Have you ever _ _ _ _ _ _ to Alaska?

2. did   I have already _ _ _ _ the project.

3. take   He has _ _ _ _ _ the three packages to the gym.

4. eat   Ursula _ _ _ two pieces of pie.

5. fall   Richard _ _ _ _ from the scaffold and didn't hurt himself.

6. ride   Neither of the boys had _ _ _ _ _ _ the horse before.

7. bring   Has he _ _ _ _ _ _ the correct information?

8. come   Kenny has _ _ _ _ forth as the party's candidate. _____.

9. begun   Lyle _ _ _ _ _ the job before the others arrived.

10. give   Others have _ _ _ _ _ much more than that.

11. see   Evelyn _ _ _ you win the highest award.

12. go   He and Tommy _ _ _ _ to the basketball game.

The American personality is _ _ _ _ _ _ _   _ _ _ _ _ _.

© 1994 by the Center for Applied Research in Education

123. "THE BRITISH ARE COMING! THE BRITISH ARE COMING!"

The *subject* of both of the above sentences is the word *British*. Use the first letter of each sentence's subject to identify a famous American and the city associated with him. Write his name and the city below the last sentence.

1. Unfortunately the price of ignorance is dear.

2. During the next hour anybody can enter the race.

3. Ulysses is a name from mythology.

4. Over the years Larry has been a winner.

5. The research of scientists contributes to many advances.

6. Existentialism is an interesting philosophy.

7. Vincent amazes a great number of people.

8. In the next few months everything will seem important.

9. Seldom has racquetball seemed so exhausting.

10. Enjoyment is a must!

11. A bouquet of flowers was delivered to my house.

12. Ornithology is the science of birds.

13. Recently the study of disease has captured my interest.

14. Most terminology confuses him.

15. Those ostriches were funny!

16. Uniquely neither of the authors was in attendance.

The famous American is _ _ _ _ _ _ _ _ _ _ and the city is _ _ _ _ _ _.

124. "I DONE GOOD!"

❧

Your English teacher's ears would ring if he or she heard you say this sentence. This activity tests your knowledge of correct usage. After selecting the correct answer for each question, cross out the corresponding number from the line of numbers at the top of this activity. The total of the six remaining digits is 32.

7 9 5 6 4 1 3 9 7 8 4 7 1 2 7 9 7 5 3 6 2

1. I could (have², of³) done it by myself.

2. She should (learn⁹, teach³) you how to tie those knots.

3. Frank has (fewer¹, less⁵) money than Bob.

4. May is shorter than (I², me⁸).

5. The musicians played (good², well⁷) at the concert.

6. Divide the goodies (among⁵, between⁹) the two of them.

7. The movie had a positive (affect¹, effect³) on the students.

8. Val sat (beside⁹, besides⁷) me at the game.

9. We couldn't find the animal (anywhere⁸, anywheres⁶).

10. He has improved his attitude (some⁶, somewhat⁵).

11. The man (who⁴, whom⁶) I introduced to you is handsome.

12. Marilyn didn't have (any⁴, no³) money.

13. The hikers still have a long (way⁹, ways²) to go before noon.

14. None of the bikers (is¹, are⁵) here yet.

15. You must (leave⁴, let⁷) me do it now!

Name _____ **Date** _____ **Period** _____

125. IS IT HE AND I OR HE AND ME?

One of the confusing aspects of usage is when to use certain pronouns. Add up the numbers below the answers you've chosen when you finish with each group. If you have selected the correct pronoun in each sentence, the totals for both groups will be the same.

GROUP ONE

A. (He and I, He and me) can do the work faster.
     1   2

B. The winners are (they, them).
           1   2

C. Hal, the boy (who, whom) you chose, is here.
           3   4

D. Is it (they, them)?
        3   4

E. Molly bought both Bob and (I, me) sneakers.
                   4 3

F. My friend and (she, her) arrived at the same time.
            4   2

Total number: _____

GROUP TWO

A. This is a secret between (she and I, her and I, her and me).
                           4   5   6

B. Take the gift to (Bob and her, Bob and she).
                4   3

C. (My sister and them, My sister and they) are happy now.
     1   2

D. He is as tall as (I, me).
              2 1

E. Neither he nor (I, me) can be there at that time.
              2 3

Total number: _____

126. "DON'T SAY, 'EACH GIRL HAS THEIR PURSE.'"

~~~

One of the most difficult usage problems involves agreement. We should say, "Each girl has her purse,"for correct agreement of pronoun and antecedent. Subject and verb agreement can also be tricky. Is the word "measles" singular or plural? This activity will help clear up some of these questions. Circle the correct word in each sentence. Then use the first letter of the correct answers to identify the names of two countries of the world.

1. Each of the students (performs, read) his own musical piece.

2. Many articles in the newspaper (are, is) interesting.

3. None of the students (punt, kicks) the ball as well as Bob.

4. All of them (increase, betters) their scores this way.

5. (Several, Nobody) have received their awards already.

6. The news of her accomplishment (touches, please) us.

7. Alex and his brothers (is, are) coming home today.

8. (Neither, Some) of the charts is here now.

9. The animals in the cage (teach, educates) one another.

10. Ken, along with his classmates, (understands, see) why it is done that way.

11. Neither Lyle nor his friends (respond, answers) promptly.

12. Either the players or their coach (tease, kids) Harold.

13. Mathematics (expands, increase) my knowledge.

14. Most of the children (yell, screams) during scary movies.

The two countries are _____ and _____.

127. CAPITAL LETTERS

Transpose the letters that should be capitalized in these sentences to the bottom of the page. If you do this correctly, you will form a quotation by a famous American poet. Good luck!

1. nicole oliver used to live in tallahassee before she moved to europe.

2. all the red sox players who live in indianapolis spoke to norman thomas hudson.

3. edna wellings loves rhode island and texas.

4. everybody watched the movie reds.

5. neither the mouse nor the cat caught ophelia's attention.

6. thomas edison, an american scientist, inspired the writer rod serling.

7. isaac newton's theories were incredible.

8. to some harvard students edgar rice is a familiar name.

9. eventually the understanding of the words, anno domini, will be more readily understood.

10. educational research foundation, an influential organization whose leading spokeswoman is roberta olsen, called their dance super tuesday.

__ _____ __ ___ _____,__

_____ __ ___ _____.

_____

128. DON'T DON'T REPEAT REPEAT YOURSELF YOURSELF

Redundancy, saying the same thing over, should be avoided whenever possible. Say what you want without adding extra words. Cross out the unnecesary or repetitive words or phrases in these sentences.

1. John left his baseball glove right here on this spot.

2. The young infant is looking at you.

3. Marilyn, the small, petite woman, is pretty.

4. His forehead looked pale above his eyelashes.

5. It was visible to our eyes that the girl was terrified.

6. The man he is the best one for the job.

7. The quartet of four people is now singing.

8. I laugh every single time I see you.

9. Never at any time will I walk that far!

10. Forever and always I will be loyal to you.

11. Glasses that hold liquids are in the closet.

12. The author who writes will be at the bookstore today.

13. A self-operating machine was installed in our dorm.

14. Pammy did the job alone by herself.

15. He also wanted to do it too.

Compose three sentences showing redundancy problems.

_____

_____

_____

© 1994 by the Center for Applied Research in Education

129. The / prō nun´ sē ā´ shan / uv / wᵾrds

Reading a word's pronunciation can be a difficult task, but not for you. Prove your skill in this area by unscrambling the word whose pronunciation is shown in the columns below. Their definitions should help you. The first answer is done for you.

A. gĭz

B. skôld

C. pär kā´

D. ĕ jis

E. hĭ ãt´ es

F. zen´ õfõ´bĕ e

G. el´ e jĕ

H. fã´ lanks´

I. kyõõ

J. rĭ

K. tõõ´ mult´

L. fy õõ´ al

Letter	Scrambled	Unscrambled	Definition
1. L	lufe	fuel	material used for heat
2. ___	eputarq	_____	theater's main floor
3. ___	uuqee	_____	a line of persons
4. ___	xlanhap	_____	a military formation
5. ___	geias	_____	protection
6. ___	iesgu	_____	false appearance
7. ___	hitsau	_____	a gap in sequence
8. ___	yleeg	_____	mournful poem
9. ___	oepbxhoina	_____	fear of foreigners
10. ___	rwy	_____	twisted; distorted
11. ___	cdsla	_____	to burn with hot liquid
12. ___	multut	_____	noisy commotion

141

130. A LETTER FROM CAMP

Poor Harold. He has written this letter to his parents about his summer camp experience. Unfortunately, he seems to have mixed up the spellings of quite a few words. Help Harold out by correcting the misspelled words in each line. Write the correct spellings on the lines below the letter.

Dear Mom and Dad,

1   Its been a while cents eye spoke to yew. Their is so much

2   to right to you about hour summer camp. The whether has been

3   beautiful this weak. Aisle begin bye telling about the animals

4   wee have hear. They're are hoarses, hairs, bares, and doughs.

5   Last knight too girls rode passed us in ther boats. They just

6   stayed out on the lake four several ours even though the

7   councilor called too them from the sure. Won of the girls, the

8   daughter of a school principle, kept waiving to the pilot of

9   a plain above her. Than she let her live preserver lose and

10   it was found by the mail camp councilor. He was all together

11   unhappy with her and gave her sum advise. Watt hee said to her

12   was knot complementary. It wasn't a pieceful seen. The morale

13   of this tail is: Don't waist thyme and no whose watching you.

14   Please right when you can.

15   Sincerrly,

16   You're sun, Harold

1. _____
2. _____
3. _____
4. _____
5. _____
6. _____
7. _____
8. _____
9. _____
10. _____
11. _____
12. _____
13. _____
14. _____
15. _____
16. _____

131. WHICH WORD IS RIGHT?

❧❧❧

Circle the correct word in each sentence.

1. Who will perform the play's next (scene, seen)?

2. He is usually (quiet, quit, quite) jovial.

3. The dog hurt (its, it's) leg while chasing the ball.

4. When the runner (passed, past) the stands, the crowd cheered.

5. How do you plan to increase team (moral, morale)?

6. The (sole, soul) survivor of the crash is his sister.

7. Do you think that the team (threw, through) the game?

8. (Whether, Weather) you do it or not is not my decision.

9. Your efforts were all in (vain, vein).

10. Do you happen to (know, no) his correct address?

11. I would (have, of) appreciated all the help.

12. Terry saved her money and bought a (stationary, stationery) bicycle.

13. Can I exchange some of my (lose, loose) change?

14. Please (set, sit) those packages here on the table.

15. We plan to (canvas, canvass) the entire region this year.

Bonus: Unscramble these twelve letters to find two words that are often confused.

ACSEANTSTESN _____ and _____.

132. WHEN TO CITE THE SITE AND ALLUDE TO THE ILLUSION

Some words are just troublesome! Select the correct word in each sentences. Unscrambling the numbered letters in each correct answer, you have the letters to spell the names of two South American countries. The first sentence is done for you.

A. (4) p o u r   Will you (poor, pore, pour) the milk now?

B. (4) _ _ _ _ _   He is (quite, quiet) tall now.

C. (5) _ _ _ _ _ _   The (amount, number) of love he has for us is plentiful.

D. (1) _ _ _ _   The (cent , sent) is a coin.

E. (1) _ _ _ _ _ _ _ _   In his book the author makes and (allusion, illusion) to Shakespeare.

F. (4) _ _ _ _ _   She has a (flair, flare) for the dramatic.

G. (4) _ _ _ _   The machine flew (good, well).

H. (3) _ _ _ _   They wanted more (meat, meet) for dinner.

I. (4) _ _ _ _ _ _ _   Because she didn't want to go to school, Patsy (fainted, feigned, feinted) illness.

J. (4) _ _ _ _ _   Is this the (right, write) turn?

K. (3) _ _ _ _   Does this procedure (seam, seem) proper?

L. (3) _ _ _ _   I felt great (pain, pane) in my left arm.

M. (3) _ _ _ _   The weather (vain, vane, vein) was inexpensive.

N. (5) _ _ _ _ _   She would like to live (their, there).

The two South American countries are _____ and _____.

133. THOSE CONFUSING WORDS!

Circle the correct word in each sentence. After some sentences there is a number. Write that letter in the correct word on the blank line below number 15. The first letter is done for you. After you've written all the letters to the corresponding numbers, unscramble them to identify three other words that are often confused.

1. How will this test (affect, effect) my average? (6)

2. When the group is (all ready, already), we can leave.

3. Each of the families had a luxurious (berth, birth) on the cruise liner. (4)

4. We read of a large (amount, number) of fatalities. (1) (5)

5. Melissa has a real (flair, flare) for skating.

6. This team has (fewer, less) spirit than last year's team. (3)

7. The (council, counsel) will meet this Wednesday. (1) (4)

8. Joe has the (medal, mettle) to face the dangerous task. (3)

9. The (seam, seem) in her dress began to split at the dance.

10. A person who is nasty is described as a (heal, heel). (2)

11. Henry needs to lose several inches around his (waist, waste).

12. Is this (your, you're) idea of a good time?

13. The company will hire a new (personal, personnel) chief. (4)

14. What's the (principal, principle) cause of war? (4) (5)

15. The smashed (pain, pane) was replaced yesterday. (4)

_____

The three words that are often confused are:

_ _ _ _, _ _ _ _ _, and _ _ _ _.

134. IS THIS DONE FORMALLY OR FORMERLY?

Match these often confused words with their correct definitions. Some are homonyms and some have similar spellings but all can be a problem to anyone learning to use English correctly.

___	1. FORMERLY	A.	previously
___	2. PRINCIPAL	B.	punctuation mark
___	3. SHONE	C.	went forward
___	4. IT'S	D.	gone by
___	5. COMMA	E.	to misplace
___	6. ITS	F.	not fancy
___	7. PASSED	G.	not noisy
___	8. CANON	H.	it is
___	9. QUITE	I.	an aircraft
___	10. PAST	J.	possessive pronoun
___	11. SHOWN	K.	most important
___	12. QUIET	L.	a large gun
___	13. LOSE	M.	rule
___	14. CANNON	N.	according to the rules
___	15. PLAIN	O.	rule of the church
___	16. LOOSE	P.	not tight
___	17. PLANE	Q.	past tense of show
___	18. COMA	R.	period of unconsciousness
___	19. FORMALLY	S.	past tense of shine
___	20. PRINCIPLE	T.	completely

135. IS A BICYCLE STATIONARY OR STATIONERY?

The English language contains some confusing words. A bicycle has to be stationary, unless of course, it is made of paper—but it wouldn't support much weight that way! Match these twenty often confused words with their correct definitions.

___ 1. STATIONARY

___ 2. DISCREET

___ 3. WEAK

___ 4. THEIR

___ 5. THROUGH

___ 6. WASTE

___ 7. EMIGRATE

___ 8. WAIST

___ 9. STATIONERY

___ 10. YOUR

___ 11. DISINTERESTED

___ 12. EULOGY

___ 13. UNINTERESTED

___ 14. WEEK

___ 15. ELEGY

___ 16. YOU'RE

___ 17. THEY'RE

___ 18. THERE

___ 19. DISCRETE

___ 20. IMMIGRATE

A. not interested

B. you are

C. owned by you

D. impartial

E. to leave one's country to go to another

F. paper

G. a place

H. dross

I. a mournful poem

J. a praise honoring a dead person

K. possessive of they

L. to come into a new country

M. by way of

N. careful

O. in a fixed position

P. not strong

Q. the lower part of the torso

R. a period of seven days

S. they are

T. separate

136. HOMOPHONES

Nineteen homophones are printed vertically under the blanks below. Match the homophone with its correct definition and insert that letter in the proper blank. After you have filled in the blanks, the word will fit the definition following the blanks. Not all of the definitions in the column will be used. The first one is done for you.

1. Q __ __ __ __ __: a mineral

   knead lieu wholly mane hangar forth

2. __ __ __ __: a translucent calcite

   hue hale feat faint

3. __ __ __ __ __: a young person

   kernel corral corps canvass coarse

4. __ __ __ __: secret dens

   dough belle urn burrow

a. all
b. hollow
c. grain of corn
d. rough
e. pretty woman
f. silent
g. deceive
h. pen for livestock
i. army unit
j. glisten
k. morbid
l. survey
m. a bread mixture
n. healthy
o. color
p. fragile
q. to mix with the hands
r. hair
s. to dig
t. storage building
u. instead of
v. friendly
w. a container
x. weak
y. accomplishment
z. forward

Bonus: Write and define the homophones for each of the words under the blanks.

© 1994 by the Center for Applied Research in Education

137. HOMONYMS—KNOWING WHEN TO USE WHAT

Don't allow the activity's title to intimidate you. Homonyms, words that sound alike but are spelled differently, can be confusing. These sentences will help to clear up some homonym problems. Circle the correct word in each sentence.

1. We could hear him (whaling, wailing) in the other room.

2. It is (their, there, they're) decision.

3. Please don't (stair, stare) in her direction.

4. They chose to spend their vacation on a beautiful (aisle, I'll, isle).

5. I will (stake, steak) all the money I have that Jerry is voted team captain.

6. Have you (read, red) all of the biology homework?

7. Do you have enough (doe, dough) to make the bread?

8. The fishing instructor told me to (real, reel) in my line when I feel a pull.

9. We plan to build the mall on this (sight, site).

10. (Weather, Whether) you go or not depends on the other members of the committee.

11. Hank chose to stay (while, wile) his dad elected to go home early.

12. Nobody (knows, nose) the route better than he.

13. Another name for the cross is the (rood, rude).

14. We saw several (dear, deer) scampering through the forest.

15. The horse's (main, mane) was beautiful.

16. Carol thought you (gnu, knew, new) the story's author.

17. You look as though you could use a few hours of (rest, wrest).

18. The police were forced to (seas, seize) the perpetrators after they had robbed the bank.

19. We certainly hope that this film does not (boar, bore) you.

20. She placed her foot on the (stile, style) in order to climb over the fence.

138. HAVEN'T I HEARD THAT BEFORE?

The twenty-five words in the first set below can be matched with a word that sounds much like itself from the second set. However, the words in the second set have been scrambled to create a greater challenge for you. Match these words with their homonyms.

FIRST SET

1. ___ see
2. ___ throne
3. ___ loan
4. ___ grown
5. ___ weal
6. ___ while
7. ___ seize
8. ___ I'll
9. ___ wait
10. ___ threw
11. ___ pair
12. ___ sheer
13. ___ hail
14. ___ might
15. ___ night
16. ___ way
17. ___ mussel
18. ___ vein
19. ___ veil
20. ___ steel
21. ___ shoe
22. ___ dear
23. ___ bough
24. ___ great
25. ___ seen

SECOND SET

a. leiw
b. inav
c. time
d. osoh
e. sliae
f. eas
g. gourhth
h. hares
i. lave
j. ghtkin
k. noel
l. gwtehi
m. reed
n. prae
o. least
p. geihw
q. hewle
r. tager
s. obw
t. lhea
u. necse
v. ases
w. scelum
x. hotrnw
y. anorg

Define each of these homonyms so you know their definitions and when each word should be used.

139. FIND THE OTHER WORD

This puzzle is full of words that are commonly misspelled or misused. Pole and poll are two examples. Find the twenty-one words and then discuss their meanings with your classmates.

```
C  O  L  L  E  G  E  T  M  H  R  F  M  F  Y  D  F  G  Y  X  F  R  V  H
Q  G  Z  Z  K  Q  Z  S  K  G  F  Q  P  R  G  K  L  G  T  T  Y  N  W  L
W  M  F  W  X  K  X  V  M  J  N  Z  R  G  T  L  F  M  T  W  V  C  D  P
D  Q  M  X  X  K  P  B  L  N  S  G  R  C  M  V  C  G  H  W  H  G  P  M
T  N  Q  T  T  X  N  K  W  B  V  S  J  G  Y  C  Z  Q  K  K  Y  G  P  L
V  X  D  M  D  C  G  G  G  W  Q  F  L  N  R  X  Z  Q  T  T  Z  B  S  K
W  Z  C  B  X  W  D  Q  W  L  V  Y  Y  W  N  T  N  Z  J  W  T  J  G  Z
M  S  D  X  F  K  L  B  V  Y  N  M  K  Z  L  B  L  R  D  D  F  S  W  Z
V  P  U  L  X  R  S  Q  R  W  N  Q  T  R  X  R  N  Q  F  V  L  P  H  Q
Y  G  R  O  X  R  Q  J  L  H  P  T  T  C  Y  Q  G  G  Z  B  T  T  D  C
B  M  H  P  R  V  H  W  P  S  R  O  N  E  J  V  D  B  P  S  J  Z  O  N
B  A  H  E  S  U  B  T  B  M  R  V  Y  T  D  E  V  P  A  W  C  L  Q  N
J  H  L  S  U  R  T  F  K  T  R  J  E  X  E  E  T  T  R  L  L  M  Y  V
J  X  Z  L  N  T  S  R  U  F  B  N  X  C  Y  N  C  I  V  A  L  D  K  L
N  W  K  I  O  P  A  O  O  V  E  H  O  Y  P  P  N  E  G  R  Y  E  T  X
T  N  A  N  E  T  U  T  A  T  S  R  E  I  N  G  I  E  R  I  N  G  T  L
G  R  K  Y  X  S  H  L  S  T  P  O  L  L  W  H  E  Y  H  P  O  L  E  B
```

1. ballet
2. ballot
3. collage
4. college
5. pole
6. poll
7. precede
8. proceed
9. rain
10. reign
11. rein
12. ring
13. statue
14. statute
15. tenant
16. tenet
17. tortuous
18. torturous
19. way
20. whey
21. wring

140. A CONFUSING CROSSWORD PUZZLE

Thirty words often confused are the answers to this crossword puzzle. Good luck!
P.S.: Don't get too confused.

ACROSS CLUES

1. a group of watchers
7. hobby
11. to think up
12. to exit
14. distinguishing between right and wrong
18. to carry to a place
21. agreement
22. result
23. through the space that separates two things
24. nativity
26. an indefinitely large number
27. harsh
28. a small island

DOWN CLUES

2. a state's seat of government
3. a group to watch or hear a play or concert
4. to perceive sounds
5. a building in the state's seat of government
6. one's employment
8. act of rising
9. to find
10. to allow
13. a liking or inclination
15. to influence
16. a ship's place of anchorage
17. a stopping device
19. surrounded by
20. a dry, sandy region
23. to carry from a place
24. an interruption or break
25. a passage between two rows

WORD LIST

AFFECT	AUDIENCE	BREAK	DISCOVER	LEAVE
AFFINITY	AVOCATION	BRING	EFFECT	LET
AISLE	BERTH	CAPITAL	HEAR	MORAL
AMONG	BETWEEN	CAPITOL	INFINITY	SPECTATORS
ASCENT	BIRTH	COARSE	INVENT	TAKE
ASSENT	BRAKE	DESERT	ISLE	VOCATION

Name _____ **Date** _____ **Period** _____

141. ARE YOU ADEPT ENOUGH TO ADAPT?

This crossword puzzle features words that are often confused. Examples such as *always* and *all ways* are just two of those included here. Once you have completed the puzzle, study the words so you will know when to correctly use these often confused words.

ACROSS CLUES

3. a single copy of a book
4. the right to enter
6. to avoid or escape detection
7. to receive willingly
8. an overabundance
13. everyone is prepared
14. unfavorable
15. to take as one's own
16. to inform or notify

DOWN CLUES

1. to refer to
2. yearly
4. to fit
5. to leave out or take out
6. to irritate greatly
7. totally
9. every way
10. act of adding
11. before or previously
12. coming twice a year
15. skilled

WORD LIST

ACCESS	ADEPT	ALLUDE	ANNUAL	ELUDE
ACCEPT	ADOPT	ALTOGETHER	APPRISE	EXCESS
ADAPT	ADVERSE	ALL WAYS	BIANNUAL	EXCEPT
ADDITION	ALL READY	ALREADY	EDITION	EXASPERATE

Section VI

Taking the Tests by the Horns

142. A BEVY OF B'S

Twenty-five words beginning with the letter b are buzzing around waiting to be trapped within your circles. The first one, "babble", is circled for you. You can find the other twenty-four. The words are placed backwards, forwards, diagonally, and up and down.

```
B U B O N I C N L C K M G N B A R B E Q U E L Y
X A D Q Z F E K B X Y Y O H J M X M W M C A M G
G Q R L F D P G V G Y O Y V B N Y C S Z C B R S
J K R R S M Q B R B R N L B L H Q M I A T C B
F Q F U A Z N Y K B Y N R L R W D H L R B V T Q
Z P B B N G C G A D L R Q P B Y J B B T P V W L
P H W Y B R E B E B F S R N R N I A D X B L T Y
L Q Z T R G P K Y L U F G Y K B R N R C B B F H
C M K S Z L S Z T L I S H Y O I H N Z S K D M M
K R J K T S G U M W F H I C A B Q B B H L N F L
W P B M B A R B E T T E P N I K S U B U B B L E
S H C S V E Y B Q A L M O O E E K U Q P C F S Q
V X N S E X O B C R N O S W I S N K B Q C Z T J
Q G B B C B L B U C L K S B J L S J X S Y R P C
D B E V B M O B E L B B A B O M B A S T I C M K
Z B Y E V B N J A N B B D W C N M I P P S C J D
B A R B E L L B U L B O U S Q B I B B E R M B T
```

BABBLE
BABBOON
BABIES
BALLOON
BARBARIAN
BARBELL
BARBEQUE

BARBETTE
BARRAGE
BEBEERU
BIBBER
BIBLICAL
BIBLIOPHILE
BOBBER

BOBCAT
BOMB
BOMBASTIC
BUBBLE
BUBONIC
BULB
BULBOUS

BURDEN
BUSBOY
BUSINESS
BUSKIN

143. FROM A TO Z

Each of the 26 letters of the alphabet provides the first letter of the answers to this crossword puzzle. The only letter that is used twice is the letter z. Have some fun as you go through the alphabet—and a bit more!

ACROSS CLUES

4. to take by force
6. rural
7. earnestness
8. action intended to outwit another person
10. wealthy
13. to wander
16. to waver back and forth
19. crazy
24. random
25. sharp or biting
26. conceited

DOWN CLUES

1. a man's wig
2. idealistic in an impractical way
3. the fourteenth letter of the Greek alphabet
5. impassive
7. gusto
9. to twist or bend
11. not clear
12. a maze
14. to long for
15. humorous
17. to ignite
18. illegal
20. a prejudiced person
21. to reveal
22. frightful
23. fertile

WORD LIST

ABSURD	FECUND	KINDLE	PLOY	USURP	ZEAL
BIGOT	GHASTLY	LABYRINTH	QUIXOTIC	VACILLATE	ZEST
CAUSTIC	HAPHAZARD	MEANDER	RUSTIC	WARP	
DIVULGE	ILLICIT	NEBULOUS	STOLID	XI	
EGOTISTICAL	JOCULAR	OPULENT	TOUPEE	YEARN	

Name _____ Date _____ Period _____

144. ARE YOU INDIFFERENT TO ANARCHY?

Indifferent and *anarchy* are two vocabulary words that have often appeared on the S.A.T. Knowing their meanings and the meanings of other words in this crossword puzzle can improve your score on the Verbal S.A.T. Fill in the letters of these often used S.A.T. words.

ACROSS CLUES

1. haughty
3. hard to capture
5. strict; severe; stern
8. pending
9. to make up a lie
12. to stop; to prevent
15. keen
17. lack of government
18. weird; out of the ordinary
19. trite; commonplace, hackneyed
21. disagreement
24. clear; easy to understand
25. lasting a short time only
26. passion

DOWN CLUES

2. unbiased
4. to spend wastefully
6. a puzzle or a mystery
7. studious; task-oriented
10. not caring one way or another
11. to admire greatly; to honor
13. to add to
14. making peace
16. yielding; submissive
20. new; a form of literature
22. serious
23. cunning; duplicity

WORD LIST

ACUTE	COMPLIANT	ELUSIVE	INDIFFERENT	SQUANDER
ANARCHY	CONCILIATORY	ENIGMA	LUCID	TENTATIVE
ARROGANT	DETER	EPHEMERAL	NEUTRAL	
AUGMENT	DILIGENT	FABRICATE	NOVEL	
AUSTERE	DISCORD	FERVOR	REVERE	
BANAL	ECCENTRIC	GUILE	SOLEMN	

159

145. RACKING UP ON THE S.A.T.

Here are twenty-two words that have appeared frequently on the S.A.T.. By studying these and other often used S.A.T. words, you can increase your score on this important test. Fill in the correct words and keep them stored in your S.A.T. memory bank.

ACROSS CLUES

4. increase; addition
5. to try in court
8. stingy
9. unfavorable
10. careful
12. mysterious
13. bulk, muscular strength
16. not believing; doubting
17. massive, solid, uniform
19. not speaking much; not liking to talk
20. a leaning towards; a strong liking
21. scarcity
22. to free from; to disentangle

DOWN CLUES

1. severe; strict; rigid
2. to assuage or mitigate
3. a joining or union
6. loyalty
7. substitute
11. bad sounding
14. seeking revenge
15. illegal
18. flowing, giving freely

WORD LIST

ADVERSE	FIDELITY	MONOLITHIC	PROFUSE	TACITURN
BRAWN	ILLICIT	PARSIMONIOUS	PRUDENT	VINDICTIVE
CACOPHONY	INCREMENT	PALLIATE	SKEPTICAL	
CRYPTIC	LITIGATE	PAUCITY	STRINGENT	
EXTRICATE	MERGER	PENCHANT	SURROGATE	

146. THE E–Z PUZZLE

If you like the letters *e* and *z,* you'll love this puzzle since every answer starts with either of these two letters. Try hard! Things should be *E-Z* for you!

ACROSS CLUES

1. thorough; leaving nothing out
3. fair
5. to call forth; extract
6. to urge
8. native
10. science dealing with animals
11. constellations
12. famous; high; lofty
13. gentle breeze
15. foolish; a foolish person
16. odd; unconventional

DOWN CLUES

1. known to a few; confidential
2. to glorify
4. learned; scholarly
6. to praise
7. mystery; riddle
9. remarkably bad
10. back-and-forth
11. musical instrument
12. to erase
13. highest point; peak; summit
14. to instruct so as to improve
15. devotion; passion

WORD LIST

ECCENTRIC	EMINENT	ESOTERIC	ZANY	ZITHER
EDIFY	ENDEMIC	EXALT	ZEAL	ZODIAC
EFFACE	ENIGMA	EXHAUSTIVE	ZENITH	ZOOLOGY
EGREGIOUS	EQUITABLE	EXHORT	ZEPHYR	
ELICIT	ERUDITE	EXTOL	ZIGZAG	

147. FIT TO A "T"

This puzzle will T's you. Don't get T'd off! Just T off and you'll be successful. Write the correct answers to this T-rific test of your knowledge.

ACROSS CLUES

1. send
3. grave; a burial monument
4. hike; a migration
6. handyman; one who mends pots and pans
7. short and to the point
8. disheveled
9. work
10. bitter speech; harangue
13. the same as; equivalent to
14. boldness

DOWN CLUES

1. belief, principle or doctrine
2. standard for determining value
3. calm; serene
4. to cross; to oppose
5. insignificant
8. moderate
9. implied
11. region; a pamphlet
12. tax
13. fall over

WORD LIST

TACIT	TERSE	TOPPLED	TRANSMIT
TANTAMOUNT	TINKER	TOUCHSTONE	TRAVAIL
TEMERITY	TIRADE	TOUSLED	TRAVERSE
TEMPERATE	TOLL	TRACT	TREK
TENET	TOMB	TRANQUIL	TRIVIAL

148. SUCCESS ON THE STANDARDIZED TESTS

Twenty words that appear often on the S.A.T. and other important tests are the answers to this puzzle. Write the correct answers in their proper spaces. So don't solemnly and stoically sit in a stationary position. Get going and be successful!

ACROSS CLUES

1. yearning; longing pensively
4. automatic
6. burn slightly
7. begin
8. flexible; lithe
9. following after
12. common; hackneyed; overused
14. scorn
17. very obvious
18. great misfortune; disaster
19. showing little or no emotion

DOWN CLUES

2. worthy of praise
3. pain; to annoy or tease
5. on time
9. standing still
10. serious; deeply earnest
11. to put down
13. crucial
15. clever
16. serene or calm

WORD LIST

BANAL
BELITTLE
CALAMITY
COMMENCE
DISDAIN
FLAGRANT
INGENIOUS

LAUDABLE
LIMBER
PACIFIC
PIVOTAL
PROMPT
SCORCH
SOLEMN

SPONTANEOUS
STATIONARY
STOIC
SUBSEQUENT
TORMENT
WISTFUL

Name _____ Date _____ Period _____

149. S.A.T. WORD UNSCRAMBLING

Forty common S.A.T. words have been scrambled here. Unscramble them and write the correct word in the adjacent blank. The word's first letter is underlined for you.

1. _____ aosihbl
2. _____ seeddnc
3. _____ euedrn
4. _____ epayjdor
5. _____ atnyrt
6. _____ eboes
7. _____ dsadicr
8. _____ shetoo
9. _____ vaegu
10. _____ wyr
11. _____ ajded
12. _____ pdeib
13. _____ dsrso
14. _____ leod
15. _____ eanbru
16. _____ samtgi
17. _____ nuorcc
18. _____ smsich
19. _____ rtyo
20. _____ usrpe

21. _____ avnshi
22. _____ wfhra
23. _____ rlaeop
24. _____ enaget
25. _____ borted
26. _____ caelev
27. _____ srhlli
28. _____ iold
29. _____ eru
30. _____ uqirk
31. _____ arachic
32. _____ dyfei
33. _____ eyegl
34. _____ eyfgif
35. _____ thessi
36. _____ laiib
37. _____ qeuip
38. _____ cduil
39. _____ tuamra
40. _____ ehtit

© 1994 by the Center for Applied Research in Education

Name _____ **Date** _____ **Period** _____

150. MANY WAYS TO SAY HAPPY

Here is a cryptogram that includes fifteen words that are synonyms for *happy*. Use the code word grid below. A little help is awaiting you there.

1. _ _ _ _ _ _ _   W O P G X P L

2. _ _ _   F G I

3. _ _ _ _ _ _ _ _   X G Z N X C N P L

4. _ _ _ _ _ _ _ _   L P O N F V Z P L

5. _ _ _ _ _   E P B B I

6. _ _ _ _ _   K J O O I

7. _ _ _ _ _ _ _ _   Z V B N O O P L

8. _ _ _ _ _ _   K J I C H O

9. _ _ _ _ _ _ _ _ _   U J Q Z P Q Z P L

10. _ _ _ _ _ _ _   Z N U A O P L

11. _ _ _ _ _ _ _ _   U V P P B C H O

12. _ _ _ _ _ _   P O G Z P L

13. _ _ _ _ _ _   K J D N G O

14. _ _ _ _ _ _   M O N Z V P

15. _ _ _ _ _ _   K J U H Q L

Real letters: A B C D E F G H I J K L M N O P Q R S T U V W X Y Z

Substitute
letters: _ _ _ _ _ C̲ _ _ _ A̲ _ _ _ _ _ _ _ _ _ _ _ _ _ _ I̲ _ _

151. A SHELTER'S SAFETY

Each of the fifteen scrambled words below are synonyms for the word *SHELTER*. Write the word next to its scrambled version. Then using the circled letters write the name of one of America's most famous shelters after the last scrambled word.

1. _ _ _ _ Ⓞ   n a v e h

2. Ⓞ _ Ⓞ _ _ _   e u e r f g

3. _ _ _ _ _ _   m l s a y u

4. _ _ _ _ Ⓞ _   r a h r b o

5. _ _ _ _ Ⓞ _ _   t u i e h d o

6. _ Ⓞ _ _ _ _   y t e s f a

7. Ⓞ _ _ _   e c a v

8. Ⓞ _ _ _ _ _   c s e s e r

9. _ _ Ⓞ _   k n o o

10. Ⓞ _ _   e d n

11. _ Ⓞ _ _ _   h c i n e

12. _ _ _   w e m

13. _ _ Ⓞ _ _ Ⓞ   t u g u d o

14. _ _ _ Ⓞ _ _ _ _   s e t o f r r s

15. _ _ _ Ⓞ _ _ _ _   h e a s f o l d

One of America's most famous shelters is _ _ _ _ _ _ _ _ _ _ _ _ _ _ _.

152. PARADISE IN OTHER WORDS

Nine words that mean *PARADISE* are found in this word grid. The letters of each word must be in a box adjacent to each other. All 54 letters in the grid will be used, but no box will be used twice. The word *VALHALLA* has already been found for you. Find the other eight and write those names below the grid.

U	O	P	O	I	Z
T	I	A	N	I	B
E	S	M	U	L	U
L	Y	I	U	E	J
D	U	M	P	S	L
A	E	Y	L	A	L
N	H	A	E	O	A
X	A	V	N	H	L
E	D	E	N	V	A

VALHALLA _____   _____   _____

_____   _____   _____

_____   _____   _____

153. FRIEND OR FOE OR NO CONNECTION?

∽✦∽

If the two words are synonyms, write S. If they're antonyms, write A. If there is no immediate connection between the two words, write NC.

1. ___ apex—summit

2. ___ furor—tranquillity

3. ___ intolerable—bearable

4. ___ duplicity—furrow

5. ___ curtail—increase

6. ___ exalt—dishonor

7. ___ laconic—wordy

8. ___ exorbitant—sheer

9. ___ altruistic—egocentric

10. ___ vogue—stylish

11. ___ haughty—humble

12. ___ exacerbate—alleviate

13. ___ epicure—connoisseur

14. ___ temper—illicit

15. ___ ingenious—hoary

16. ___ thwart—aid

17. ___ fecund—unproductive

18. ___ noisome—offensive

19. ___ insensible—impassive

20. ___ fundamental—warp

21. ___ reclusive—outgoing

22. ___ integrity—dishonesty

23. ___ guileful—cunning

24. ___ uniqueness—ultimate

25. ___ obdurate—flexible

26. ___ shrill—acute

27. ___ paucity—ploy

28. ___ tantalize—repel

29. ___ lavish—cheap

30. ___ feasible—tawdry

31. ___ obliterate—erect

32. ___ enigma—mystery

33. ___ esoteric—diligent

34. ___ eradicate—inscribe

35. ___ martinet—shrew

36. ___ nonentity—maudlin

154. GREAT HANGMAN WORDS

Hangman, a game in which your opponent is asked to guess your word letter by letter, is fun and educational. Here are twenty-five Hangman classics. Match the words with their definitions.

byte	gypsum	mnemonic	queue	usury
dyad	gyro	myrrh	quixotic	vex
eke	hype	nth	rhythm	whelp
faze	kayak	phlegm	tryst	whey
gym	lymph	phylum	unctuous	zinc

1. _____ redezvous

2. _____ line

3. _____ the highest degree

4. _____ beat

5. _____ idealistic but impractical

6. _____ fragrant gum used in perfumes

7. _____ division of animal kingdom

8. _____ lending of money at a very high interest

9. _____ a member of the periodic table

10. _____ thick mucus

11. _____ watery part of milk

12. _____ place for exercise

13. _____ pair

14. _____ Eskimo canoe

15. _____ a string of binary units

16. _____ helping the memory

17. _____ excessive promotion

18. _____ fatty; oily

19. _____ annoy

20. _____ disturb

21. _____ occurring naturally in sedimentary rock

22. _____ a sandwich made with lamb

23. _____ cub

24. _____ to make out in scanty fashion

25. _____ a clear, yellowish fluid

155. PHOBOPHOBIA

❧

When Franklin D. Roosevelt said, "The only thing we have to fear is fear itself," he was refer-ring to phobophobia, the fear of fear. Here are some other types of fears. On the line write the letter of the fear that best fits the proper quotation. Each is used only once.

a. agoraphobia
b. androphobia
c. arachnephobia
d. cardiophobia
e. claustrophobia

f. ergophobia
g. gynephobia
h. hemophobia
i. hydrophobia
j. logophobia

k. neophobia
l. nyctophobia
m. toxicophobia
n. triskaidekaphobia
o. xenophobia

1. _____ "Women intimidate me!"

2. _____ "Keep that daddy longlegs away from me!"

3. _____ "I don't want to see another word!"

4. _____ "Poisonous foods will be the death of me!"

5. _____ "I don't want to meet any strangers!"

6. _____ "I'll need at least three life preservers."

7. _____ "Don't lock me in that small room!"

8. _____ "Don't dare introduce me to a man!"

9. _____ "My heart will not last much longer!"

10. _____ "I wish there were 24 hours of daylight."

11. _____ "Thirteen…Thirteen…Thirteen!"

12. _____ "Nothing new for me!"

13. _____ "I'll faint if I see blood!"

14. _____ "If I work, I'll probably die!"

15. _____ "I hate public places!"

156. SAME OR OPPOSITE?

The words in the twenty analogies below are either synonyms or antonyms of each other. Write the letter S for synonym or A for antonym next to the pair of words. The first letters of the first word of those pairs that are synonyms will spell the name of a famous British author. Write the author's name below the last pair.

1. ___ entice—lure

2. ___ long-lasting—ephemeral

3. ___ slothful—ambitious

4. ___ martinet—pushover

5. ___ mollify—sooth

6. ___ burgeon—wither

7. ___ inherent—intrinsic

8. ___ lament—mourn

9. ___ heinous—honorable

10. ___ glib—inarticulate

11. ___ yen—desire

12. ___ seraphic—demonic

13. ___ banal—commonplace

14. ___ tentative—definite

15. ___ reticent—quiet

16. ___ obscure—not clear

17. ___ agile—clumsy

18. ___ nebulous—vague

19. ___ tacit—not spoken

20. ___ exculpate—exonerate

The famous British author is _ _ _ _ _ _ _ _ _ _ _.

Name _____ **Date** _____ **Period** _____

157. S.A.T. ANALOGY QUESTIONS

An analogy is a relationship that shows a parallel between two sets of words. A typical analogy is, *"Son is to father is the same as daughter is to mother."* Seven of the most common analogies found on the S.A.T. are found below. Match the pair of words with the correct relationship by writing the corresponding letter. The first is done for you.

ANALOGY TYPE

A. Synonym

B. Antonym

C. Part is to Whole

D. Intensity or Degree

E. Type of

F. Order (sequence)

G. Sign of

EXAMPLE

display : exhibit

high : low

motor : automobile

lukewarm : hot

pen : writing implement

adolescence : adulthood

tears : sorrow

1. ___ cornea : eye

2. ___ miniscule : small

3. ___ picture : montage

4. ___ dislike : hatred

5. ___ interest : obsession

6. ___ dancer : performer

7. ___ novel : literature

8. ___ impolite : rude

9. ___ act : play

10. ___ arc : circle

11. ___ brag : conceited

12. ___ virus : illness

13. ___ clap : approval

14. ___ apple : fruit

15. ___ knee : leg

16. ___ acme : nadir

158. S.A.T. ANALOGIES MATCHUP

Using a sentence to state the relationship of an analogy helps to improve your S.A.T. score. Match each of these twelve analogies with the sentence that best states the relationship. Refer to the first word in each pair as A and the second as B. If your answers are correct, you will find two girls' names within the answer column. Circle their names.

A. misdemeanor : crime

B. director : cast

C. cry : sadness

D. neophyte : veteran

E. cardiologist : heart

F. expel : pupil

G. neigh : horse

H. warm : torrid

I. mediator : quarrel

J. myopia : nearsightedness

K. egomaniac : brag

L. monument : commemorate

1. ___ A is the sound made by B

2 ___ A is the small type of B

3. ___ A attempts to settle B

4. ___ The purpose of A is to B

5. ___ If I do A, I show B

6. ___ A is not as intense as B

7. ___ A and B are opposites

8. ___ A is one who treats B

9. ___ A leads B

10. ___ A is how B is ousted

11. ___ A often does B

12. ___ A and B are the same

159. S.A.T. COMPLETIONS...THE DEFINITIONS

One type of S.A.T. question is the sentence completion. In the exercise below, select a word that is "defined" within the sentence. An example of this is, "Lester could be called a (n) _____ since he attacked images held sacred by others." The word *iconoclast* fits well because it is almost "defined" by the other words in the sentence. Fill in these blanks with your own words and be ready to support your choices.

1. One should not attempt to _____ others, lying to them for one's own selfish reasons.

2. A generous _____, Nancy gives generously to many worthy causes.

3. If a speaker is _____, repeating the same facts and details, he tends to bore and even annoy people.

4. She was so _____ that instead of planning out her actions, she rushed into things.

5. The task was quite _____ requiring great care and detail.

6. _____ speeches tend to put listeners to sleep.

7. The group involved itself in _____ operations concealing much from the public's curious eye.

8. The spy's _____ message could not be deciphered.

9. Showing no interest in anything academic, the _____ student could not get excited about any subject.

10. His crime was considered a(n) _____, not a capital offense.

© 1994 by the Center for Applied Research in Education

160. S.A.T. SENTENCE COMPLETIONS...
COMPLETING THE IDEA

~~~

One type of S.A.T. question is the sentence completion in which you are asked to select a word that keeps the sentence's thought or idea going in the "same" direction. An example of this is, "Because Jill is a(n) _____ student, she earns high grades." Since Jill earns *high* grades, the blank should be filled in with a *positive* word. Words such as *diligent, outstanding,* or *exemplary* work well. Fill in these blanks with your own words and be ready to support your choices.

1. Since you have performed so _____, you won first place.

2. The students elected you because of your_____record.

3. In order to complete the task, you must work _____.

4. The music was so _____ that our ears were ringing.

5. Knowing that the political rally could be _____, the speakers were asked to choose their words carefully.

6. Some celebrities are, by nature, quite shy; therefore, they will generally be _____ to granting interviews.

7. Her friends described her personalty to be _____ since they couldn't predict what she would do next.

8. Due to the _____ climate, the plants grew heartily.

9. The youngster was _____ since he had never seen something as horrific as that before.

10. Relishing the opportunity, Lyle was _____ to enter the contest.

161. S.A.T. SENTENCE COMPLETIONS...
REVERSING THE IDEA

In S.A.T. sentence completion questions, you must select a word that "reverses" the sentence's thought or idea. An example of this is, "Though Hal is a_____boy, he is not a *good* student." Words such as *smart, intelligent,* and *gifted* work well in the blank. Fill in the blanks with your own words and be ready to support your choices.

1. Although we felt the group is generally _____, we must still be cautious in dealing with them.

2. Despite the critics' scathing reviews, the book sold _____.

3. Even though Mort's science project was neat and well written, he received a(n) _____ grade on it.

4. The company's traffic record has usually been nearly perfect, but this year the record is _____.

5. Unlike others in similar positions, this director is a(n) _____, breaking all the rules of drama.

6. To Christine, baking was _____; her neighbor, however, saw baking as a(n) _____ way to pass time.

7. John is usually a(n) _____ musician but sometimes he is _____.

8. _____, yet _____, Florence is an enigmatic person.

9. Even though the scientists claim that smoking is _____, people today still _____ cigarettes.

10. Petra did not learn to ski in a week; on the contrary, it took her _____.

162. UNSCRAMBLED MEATS BECOME STEAM!

If you read this headline in the newspaper, you would think the impossible had occurred. This is not an impossibility though when it comes to rearranging a word's letters to make other words. Thus the word "meats" can easily become "steam" by rearranging the letters. See how many of the following words you can rearrange to make words that fit the definitions. The first one is done for you.

1. horse...   s h o r e   (a sandy beach)

2. tones...   _ _ _ _ _   (rock)

3. slip...   _ _ _ _   (a speech impediment)

4. strew...   _ _ _ _ _   (twist)

5. anger...   _ _ _ _ _   (stove)

6. angle...   _ _ _ _ _   (hallowed spirit)

7. elbow...   _ _ _ _ _   (under)

8. large...   _ _ _ _ _   (royal)

9. stake...   _ _ _ _ _   (beef)

10. least...   _ _ _ _ _   (rob)

11. wasp...   _ _ _ _   (to trade)

12. resign...   _ _ _ _ _ _   (one who pens his name)

13. settler...   _ _ _ _ _ _ _   (ABC's)

14. tracer...   _ _ _ _ _ _   (one who transports)

15. grown...   _ _ _ _ _   (incorrect)

16. glean...   _ _ _ _ _   (sharp corner)

17. dreaded...   _ _ _ _ _ _ _   (computed again)

18. saber...   _ _ _ _ _   (more degrading)

19. mash...   _ _ _ _   (fraud)

20. waste...   _ _ _ _ _   (to perspire heavily)

177

163. WHEN A WORD BECOMES A WARD

The changing of one letter in a word can give that word a whole new meaning. When an o is changed to an a, a word becomes a ward. See how many you can change in the list below, by writing a new letter in the circle in the newly defined word. The first one is done for you. After you have placed the new letters in their proper places, use nine of them to find a boy's first and last name. His first name is a city in Indiana and his last name means rapid!

1. C O M P O S E	to write, to make	
C O M P O S Ⓣ	fertilizer	
2. _ _ _ _ _ _ _	to cower	
_ _ Ⓞ _ _ _ _	a tiny flow of water	
3. _ _ _ _ _	rent	
_ _ _ _ Ⓞ	a strap	
4. _ _ _ _	without feeling	
Ⓞ _ _ _	silent	
5. _ _ _ _ _	beef	
_ Ⓞ _ _ _	express orally	
6. _ _ _ _ _	wed	
Ⓞ _ _ _ _	delay	
7. _ _ _ _ _	chubby	
_ _ _ _ Ⓞ	weight on the line's end	
8. _ _ _ _	twilight	
Ⓞ _ _ _	substance used in perfumes	
9. _ _ _ _ _	group of trees	
_ _ Ⓞ _ _	serious, solemn	
10. _ _ _ _ _	shelter	
Ⓞ _ _ _ _	an expert	

11. _ _ _ _ _	banquet	
Ⓞ _ _ _ _	leaven	
12. _ _ _ _ _	a popular way to communicate in the Swiss Alps	
Ⓞ _ _ _ _	mannequin	
13. _ _ _ _ _	pretend	
Ⓞ _ _ _ _	rule as a sovereign	
14. _ _ _ _ _	a knot in a tree	
Ⓞ _ _ _ _	tangle	
15. _ _ _ _ _	terry cloth dryer	
Ⓞ _ _ _ _	a letter that is not a consonant	
16. _ _ _ _ _ _	one who severs	
Ⓞ _ _ _ _ _	object for channeling water	
17. _ _ _ _ _ _	bother, annoy	
Ⓞ _ _ _ _ _	to generate pus	
18. _ _ _ _ _ _	fat used to make candles	
Ⓞ _ _ _ _ _	move heavily and clumsily	

Bonus: The boy's name is _ _ _ _ _ _ _ _ _.

Section VII

Just Plain Fun

164. AND THE CATEGORY IS...

This game will provide much fun and knowledge at the same time. Create a grid like the one below. Select five letters of the alphabet and put them in the vertical column to the left of the grid. Then select five categories and write them in the horizontal column. The object is to create an answer for that category that begins with that letter. In the grid below, the category *AUTHORS* in the letter *S* column could be filled in with Shakespeare, Salinger, Saroyan or a number of other authors. A player who is the only one with that answer gets three points, two players who have that answer get two points, and if more than two players have the answer, each receives one point. There are no deductions for blanks. You are allowed one free space. The winner is the one who accumulates the most points.

Below the grid are other possible categories. Use these or any other you can find. Have fun!

	Animals	Authors	Sports	U.S. Cities	Girls' Names
S		Shakespeare			
T					
A			auto racing		
R	rabbit			Richmond, Virginia	
E			free		Ellen

Other possible categories include:

artists	*countries*	*literary characters*	*presidents*
attire	*diseases*	*literary terms*	*religions*
authors' themes	*elements*	*magazines*	*sciences*
bodies of water	*historical figures*	*movie titles*	*states*
body parts	*land formations*	*musical performers*	*television shows*
cars	*languages*	*occupations*	

165. BIG AND SMALL

‿❧‿

How many names or expressions can you think of that contain the words big or small in them? The Big Dipper (the constellation), Big Blue (IBM), and small talk (light conversation) are just three of the many waiting to be found. Write your answers in the spaces provided. Discuss your answers with your classmates.

1. _____

2. _____

3. _____

4. _____

5. _____

6. _____

7. _____

8. _____

9. _____

10. _____

11. _____

12. _____

13. _____

14. _____

15. _____

16. _____

17. _____

18. _____

19. _____

20. _____

21. _____

22. _____

23. _____

24. _____

25. _____

166. BUILDING BLOCKS CONTEST

Get yourself ready for some fun competition. Here are twenty sets of three-letter combinations that will be used to build larger words. Use the letters in each of the 20 combinations to construct larger words. *These three letters can be found anywhere in the word as long as they are in the order they appear on this sheet.* Set a time limit of maybe four minutes to construct as many five- (or more) letter words as possible. Compare your answers with those of your classmates. If you have a word that no other student has, give yourself one point. Proper nouns and plurals are not allowed. Write your answers on a separate sheet. An example is provided for you.

Example: plt. . . pleat, complete, playtime, playsuit, simpleton

1. irt	5. tem	9. hoe	13. ete	17. enr
2. der	6. age	10. net	14. ore	18. ane
3. pen	7. ear	11. ral	15. ink	19. ant
4. ora	8. sot	12. era	16. ari	20. lim

Bonus: Expand the building Block contest to include four letters.

167. CAN YOU MAKE A WILLOW WALLOW?

The answer to this question is, "Yes!" All you need to do is change the letter i to the letter a and you have made a willow wallow! Here are sixteen more challenges for you. Change one letter in the first word to make a new word that fits the second word's definition.

1. _ _ _ _ _ _: have faith

   _ _ _ _ _ _: assuage

2. _ _ _ _ _: royal headdress

   _ _ _ _ _: perish in water

3. _ _ _ _ _: partly frozen rain

   _ _ _ _ _: any broad surface

4. _ _ _ _ _: color

   _ _ _ _ _: throughout the time that

5. _ _ _ _ _ _: a skilled person

   _ _ _ _ _ _: to assemble for roll call

6. _ _ _ _ _: group of trees

   _ _ _ _ _: valuable discovery

7 _ _ _ _ _: lid

   _ _ _ _ _: hang about

8. _ _ _ _: one who annoys

   _ _ _ _: keen enjoyment

9. _ _ _ _ _ _: fear

   _ _ _ _ _ _: radiant

10. _ _ _ _ _ _: endure pain

    _ _ _ _ _ _: something that eases the shock of a blow

11. _ _ _ _ _ _ _: gruesome

    _ _ _ _ _ _ _: like a spirit

12. _ _ _ _: quantity of paper

    _ _ _ _: interpreting language's characters

13. _ _ _ _ _ _ _ _ _ _: extreme poverty

    _ _ _ _ _ _ _ _ _ _: amends

14. _ _ _ _ _ _: empty

    _ _ _ _ _ _: consecrate

15. _ _ _ _ _ _: associate

    _ _ _ _ _ _: make sweet and gentle by age

16. _ _ _ _ _: spice

    _ _ _ _ _: near

Bonus: By changing the first letter of a word with consecutive letters of the alphabet, come up with three words whose definitions are:

_ _ _ _ to crease

_ _ _ _ a precious metal

_ _ _ _ to seize or clutch

© 1994 by the Center for Applied Research in Education

168. CATCHING SOME Z'S

This activity is not intended to put you to sleep even though you are going to catch some z's. In fact, you can catch double z's since each of the words you're asked to unscramble contains a double z combination. Definitions are given to help you along. Don't get caught napping! Instead unscramble these thirteen double z words. Besides having a double z combination, what other spelling pattern is common to all thirteen words? Write your answer below number thirteen.

1. _____ zzmleu — the front end of a firearm

2. _____ zzlepu — to confuse

3. _____ zzlaref — fray

4. _____ zzonel — the spout at the end of a hose

5. _____ zzifle — to make a hissing sound

6. _____ zzidlre — to rain lightly

7. _____ zzmleeeb — to take money fraudulently

8. _____ zzslei — to be extremely hot

9. _____ zzebadle — to bewilder

10. _____ zzrlefi — to make crisp by boiling

11. _____ zzeulg — to drink greedily

12. _____ zzlear — half of a term meaning a flashy display

13. _____ zzlead — to be overpowered by glare

Besides having a double z combination, what other spelling pattern is common to all thirteen words? _____

169. COMBINING WORDS

This activity will stir your gray matter. In each instance the two words in Column B should be combined to make a single word. So *wing* plus *ring* will be combined to make *wringing*. Good luck in combining these challenging sets of words. Write your answer in the space provided in Column A. If you would like to know the combined word's first letter, look to the extreme right of each question.

COLUMN A	COLUMN B	
1. _____	sting + art	1. s
2. _____	slash + bite	2. e
3. _____	fled + aunt	3. f
4. _____	reed + sort	4. r
5. _____	lob + gal	5. g
6. _____	per + and	6. p
7. _____	shed + are	7. s
8. _____	at + lent	8. l or t
9. _____	rid + bled	9. b
10. _____	rag + France	10. f
11. _____	row + thing	11. t
12. _____	west + arm	12. w
13. _____	dive + at	13. d
14. _____	rob + pate	14. p
15. _____	early + nest	15. e

170. A COMMON LETTER

Add the same letter to each of the group's three words to make three new words. Thus, if you add the letter G to love, land and lobe, you have glove, gland, and globe. The letter s is not permitted.

LETTER	OLD WORDS	NEW WORDS
1. _____	rot, fed, lose	_____
2. _____	lien, shoe, roe	_____
3. _____	boom, dove, cat	_____
4. _____	lame, deer, lag	_____
5. _____	sank, tang, sore	_____
6. _____	east, dad, deco	_____
7. _____	diva, doze, sped	_____
8. _____	cone, ream, dot	_____
9. _____	able, reap, mine	_____
10. _____	glad, star, rub	_____
11. _____	saner, hie, grin	_____
12. _____	war, spur, ease	_____
13. _____	tar, pat, last	_____
14. _____	ame, gale, room	_____

171. CUTTING WORDS DOWN

How fair are you when it comes to cutting down words to make new ones? Start with the word *growing* and delete one letter at a time so that what is left is still a word. The pattern looks like this: growing, rowing, owing, wing, win, in, i. Here are fifteen other words to make new words from. Proper names are allowed. Write your answers next to the original word.

1. DRAIN _____

2. SHORT _____

3. GRAND _____

4. AMORALLY _____

5. BLEND _____

6. FEAST _____

7. SPRITE _____

8. CHASTE _____

9. STILLED _____

10. WANDER _____

11. SHRED _____

12. SPRINT _____

13. TRAIL _____

14. GLOBE _____

Bonus: Name five words that fit this pattern.

© 1994 by the Center for Applied Research in Education

172. FUN WITH WORDS

This activity is not for the weak of heart. It challenges you to deal with ten questions related to the words in the columns below. Fill in the correct words in the appropriate spaces.

| caper | gaga | grapple | mundane | scatter |
| emulate | gherkin | leper | racecar | settle |

1. _____ this word is palindromic

2. _____ it contains a Muslim title of respect

3. _____ add a letter and you have an American city

4. _____ drop a letter from this and you have the equivalent of a female's relatives

5. _____ eliminate this word's vowels and you can save a life with what's left

6. _____ if you cross out every other letter of this word, you have a word meaning to stare with open mouth

7. _____ by changing this word's second letter and replacing it with another, you can make at least four other words

8. _____ this word contains a nationality

9. _____ rearrange this word's letters and you're left with a disabled American Indian

10. _____ spelled backwards, this word means the opposite of attract

173. HIDDEN WORDS

Twenty words that match the definitions below are hidden in these sentences. Underline the twenty words and then write the corresponding letter next to the sentence's number. The first one is already done for you.

a. immature
b. an organ in a flower
c. to be filled with longing
d. vow
e. falling away from a condition

f. not native
g. wage
h. oneness
i. end
j. to impose a fine

k. to think up
l. to begin
m. to commit a sin
n. to flow slowly
o. printed sign

1. _i_ Since the dolphin's fin is hurt, he cannot swim properly.

2. ___ Before igniting the fire, stand far enough away from it.

3. ___ The hotel has the best amenities money can buy!

4. ___ When the pressure is off, end this argument with your partner.

5. ___ We saw the building collapse at about three o'clock.

6. ___ The star tennis player is handsome.

7. ___ Stick the decal lower than that on your car's side window.

8. ___ Much of the factory's inventory is stored in this building.

9. ___ John's trick led to a big argument with his older brother.

10. ___ As sessions became longer, the committee did less creative work.

11. ___ Henry believed that having no tic enabled him to function better.

12. ___ He hardly earns enough money to pay his monthly bills.

13. ___ Each of the prisoners was given perpetual immunity.

14. ___ As we are, we can never win the championship.

15. ___ The waiter's tip ended up on the floor.

174. THE INITIALS GAME

❧❧❧

Here is a way to increase your knowledge of people and have fun at the same time. After the sets of initials, write the names of famous people from any walk of life. Musicians, scientists, authors, actresses, and media personalities are just a few of the many types of famous people you can select. Fill in as many of these initials as you can, and be ready to tell how this person is famous. The person or team with the most correct answers wins. The answer must be a famous person in the eyes of most of the class members. Some names are listed here to get you started.

You may want to add rule variations as you gain more experience in playing the game. Obviously, you may not always be able to find a famous person to match the initials.

If you'd like to construct your own game, begin with the alphabet in the first column and then select a line from a paper or series of words in the second column. In this game, the second column is Benjamin Franklin's proverb, "A penny saved is a penny earned." The letter t was added to make twenty-six letters.

AA	Alan Alda (actor)
BP	Boris Pasternak (author)
CE	Cass Elliot (member of the Mamas and the Papas singing group)
DN	Don Nelson (N.B.A. coach)
EN	Eliot Ness (gangster)
FY	Frank Yerby (author)
GS	Gale Storm (actress)
HA	Hank Aaron (baseball player)
IV	(Your turn!)
JE	Julius Erving (basketball player)
KD	Keir Dullea (actor)
LI	(Your Turn!)
MS	Mary Stewart (author)
NA	Nancy Astor (British politician)
OP	Oliver Perry (U.S. Navy captain)
PE	Phil Esposito (hockey player)
QN	(Your Turn!)
RN	Ricky Nelson (singer)
SY	Susannah York (actress)
TE	Tommy Edwards (singer)
UA	Ursula Andress (actress)
VR	Vanessa Redgrave (actress)
WN	Willie Nelson (singer)
XE	(Your Turn!)
YD	Yvonne DeCarlo (actress)
ZT	Zachary Taylor (U.S. President)

175. JUST HORSIN' AROUND

Each of the seventeen words is missing a two-letter combination. Select the correct combination and insert it in the appropriate word. Each combination is used only once. When you have inserted the letter combinations correctly, write the letters in order beneath the last question. Then this activity's title makes sense!

ac	be	es	ky	ne	on	re	tr	yp
ak	de	ke	lm	nt	rb	ss	uc	

1. to___n

2. me___ion

3. st___k

4. tric___

5. pru___nt

6. ba___ed

7. c___ress

8. ar___st

9. ste___

10. u___ven

11. fruitle___

12. pro___

13. rea___

14. bat___

15. en___ap

16. ___cessory

17. ___tablish

The letters written in order are:

_ _ _ _ _ _ _ _ _ _ _ _ _, _ _ _ _ _ _ _ _ _,_ _ _ _ _ _ _ _ _ _ _ _.

176. THE LETTER LINEUP

Eighteen words are hidden in this letter lineup. The definitions of these words are written below. Write the correct word next to its definition. Words are written both backwards and forward.

T L I K C A T A S T R O P H E L I A R M O R T U B A D

1. _____ a type of turf found in ballparks

2. _____ a household pet

3. _____ one who does not tell the truth

4. _____ a musical instrument

5. _____ a masculine third-person pronoun

6. _____ Hamlet's girl

7. _____ past tense of sit

8. _____ a three-letter conjunction

9. _____ body protection used in war

10. _____ a side of a ship

11. _____ the fence surrounding the infield of a racetrack

12. _____ a pleated skirt reaching to the knees

13. _____ the opposite of good

14. _____ to border on

15. _____ to be in poor health

16. _____ a short nail or pin

17. _____ large open container used for washing

18. _____ a calamity or disaster

177. LOOKING FOR SOME FUN?

Want to add some fun to your life? Each of the twenty answers contains the word FUN in it though the letters may have other letters inserted between them (as in the word *flunk*.) The letters that make up the defined word in each question are provided. All you do is add FUN to it and write your answer in the space next to the number! The first one is done for you.

1. <u>FUNNEL</u>   NEL... cone-shaped device used for pouring

2. _____   RED... repay

3. _____   DAMENTAL... essential

4. _____   AFLECE... wealth

5. _____   CTION... special purpose

6. _____   ERAL... ceremony of burial

7. _____   YK... unconventional

8. _____   ODATION... supporting structure

9. _____   OD... located

10. _____   DECT... no longer in existence

11. _____   RACE... enclosed area where heat is produced

12. _____   RITURE... equipment

13. _____   RADULET... deceitful

14. _____   OTAIN... a spring

15. _____   LODER... a fish

16. _____   D... a sum of money

17. _____   ECD... fertile

18. _____   NY... humorous

19. _____   GUS... molds, mildew, mushrooms

20. _____   INLECE... to have an effect on

Name _____ Date _____ Period _____

178. THE MONTHS OF THE YEAR

Twenty words containing the twelve months' abbreviations are used in this word identification exercise. With the help of the abbreviations, identify as many words as you can. The first one is done for you. Then unscramble the circled letters to identify the person after whom the seventh month of the year is named.

1. J A N I T O R : custodial engineer

2. M Y _ _ _ ○ : lack of understanding of foresight

3. A ○ G _ _ : prophet; soothsayer

4. J ○ N _ _ _ : the third year of high school

5. N O V _ ○ _ : beginner

6. O C T _ _ _ _ : an eight sided figure

7. ○ E P T _ _ : a group of seven persons of things

8. _ A P R _ _ ○ _ _ ○ : inconstant or erratic

9. J E _ _ ○ : a valuable ring, necklace, or pin

10. J U L _ _ : a mixture of water with syrup or sugar

11. F E B ○ _ _ _ : feverish

12. M ○ R _ _ _ _ _ : a strict disciplinarian

13. D E C _ _ ○ : to choose

14. _ _ _ _ _ MAR _ : a frightening dream

15. _ _ _ _ MY : being married to more than one spouse at the same time

16. _ _ N O V _ _ _ : to introduce new methods

17. _ _ A U G _ _ _ _ _ : to induct an official into office

18. _ O C T _ _ : physician

19. D E C _ _ _ : a period of ten years

20. ○ A N _ _ _ : to quarrel or argue noisily

The name found in the circled letters is _ _ _ _ _ _ _ _ _ _ _ _.

179. MOVE ALONG, LITTLE LETTER!

The letter t certainly gets around. Here the letter will move one spot with each new word so it starts in the first position and by the time it reaches the last word, number thirteen, it is in the thirteenth slot. The definitions and a few other letters given within the words should help you identify the correct word.

1. T _ _ : five plus five

2. _ T U _ : to daze

3. A _ T _ _ _ : to be present at

4. M _ _ T _ _ _ _ : to treat wrongly

5. C _ _ _ T _ _ : in a confused condition

6. M _ _ _ _ T _ : title used for a sovereign

7. A _ _ _ _ _ T : stubborn

8. _ Y _ _ _ M _ T _ C : made according to a plan or method

9. _ _ G _ _ _ _ A T E : a minor official with limited judicial powers

10. R _ _ E _ _ _ E _ T : a feeling of displeasure and indignation

11. _ O _ _ _ _ D _ E _ T : a mandate

12. R _ _ R _ _ _ H _ _ _ T : a reduction of expenses

13. G _ _ _ D _ L _ _ _ _ _ T : using bombastic words and expressions

Bonus: What five-letter word has three t's in it and means shabby or decrepit?

_____

Name _____   **Date** _____   **Period** _____

180. OLD AGE IS IN!

Find at least twenty words containing the word OLD and the same for the word AGE. Good luck!

OLD

1. _____	6. _____	11. _____	16. _____
2. _____	7. _____	12. _____	17. _____
3. _____	8. _____	13. _____	18. _____
4. _____	9. _____	14. _____	19. _____
5. _____	10. _____	15. _____	20. _____

AGE

1. _____	6. _____	11. _____	16. _____
2. _____	7. _____	12. _____	17. _____
3. _____	8. _____	13. _____	18. _____
4. _____	9. _____	14. _____	19. _____
5. _____	10. _____	15. _____	20. _____

181. NO P'S PLEASE!

∾⌒⌒∾

Here are twenty-five words that have had the letter p deleted. A word may need more than one letter p. Write the word with the p's reinserted in the space provided.

1. _____ eer
2. _____ assort
3. _____ aer
4. _____ reie
5. _____ arika
6. _____ ayrus
7. _____ aaya
8. _____ flaer
9. _____ aendage
10. _____ beeer
11. _____ coer
12. _____ uer
13. _____ caer
14. _____ wier
15. _____ eoxy
16. _____ cree
17. _____ relica
18. _____ roeller
19. _____ oosition
20. _____ foish
21. _____ zier
22. _____ esin
23. _____ lymh
24. _____ hay
25. _____ exress

182. A PAGE OF SINS

Find at least twenty words that include the word *sin* in them. It is no sin to find more than twenty! Good luck.

1. _____	6. _____	11. _____	16. _____
2. _____	7. _____	12. _____	17. _____
3. _____	8. _____	13. _____	18. _____
4. _____	9. _____	14. _____	19. _____
5. _____	10. _____	15. _____	20. _____

Now define ten of these words by writing their definitions below.

WORD   **DEFINITION**

1. _____   _____

2. _____   _____

3. _____   _____

4. _____   _____

5. _____   _____

6. _____   _____

7. _____   _____

8. _____   _____

9. _____   _____

10. _____   _____

183. SDRAWKCAB SDROW

Please don't feel as though you need to go for an eye examination. Your eyesight is just fine. Your eyes will come in very handy in this activity that asks you to identify the defined words. The trick is that each pair of defined words is the other word spelled backwards. The first one is done for your. DOOG KCUL!

1. <u>door</u> entranceway   <u>rood</u> cross

2. _____ celestial body   _____ rodents

3. _____ market   _____ streetcar

4. _____ mammal   _____ cane used in wind instruments

5. _____ portion   _____ snare

6. _____ give money in payment   _____ device for measuring time

7. _____ chamber   _____ to anchor

8. _____ Satan   _____ resided

9. _____ pierce   _____ mouselike mammals with wings

10. _____ to boil slowly   _____ moistens

11. _____ indentifier   _____ to fortify again

12. _____ to fuel up again   _____ wiser

13. _____ kettles and pans   _____ arrest

14. _____ box in a bureau   _____ compensation

15. _____ bar used as a pry   _____ to celebrate

16. _____ hollow stalk of grain   _____ growths on the skin

A Bonus with international appeal: Following the same idea as above, what singular form of the word meaning territorial unit in English, when reversed, is its French counterpart in plural? _____ _____

184. SOME MORE OF A NUMBER OF THINGS

Here are some equations that will make your mind work hard. If you know that 9 = N. of P. in the U. (9 is the number of planets in the universe), you will do just fine in this exercise. Solve these twenty number problems.

1. _____ 76 = T. led the B.P.

2. _____ 60 = M. in an H.

3. _____ 4 = S. in a Y.

4. _____ 2001 = S.O.

5. _____ 57 = H.V.

6. _____ 12 = D. of C.

7. _____ 7 = D. in a W.

8. _____ 13 = O.C.

9. _____ 12 = I. in a F.

10. _____ 1760 = Y. in a M.

11. _____ 24 = H. in a D.

12. _____ 12 = T. of I.

13. _____ 100 = Y. in a C.

14. _____ 1000 = Y. in a M.

15. _____ 3.14 = P.

16. _____ 14 = L. in a S.

17. _____ 2 = N. in a D.

18. _____ 14 = D. in a F.

19. _____ 10 = Y. in a D.

20. _____ 20 = Y. in a S.

185. THERE'S A LIE IN EVERY ONE OF THESE!

❧

Each of the words in the first column has the word LIE within it. Match each up with its correct definition.

1. ___ lien   A. colder than

2. ___ belie   B. help or aid

3. ___ believe   C. willingly

4. ___ collie   D. French dramatist

5. ___ relief   E. sooner than

6. ___ earlier   F. legal claim on property

7. ___ lilies   G. more foolish

8. ___ pliers   H. French-Canadian explorer

9. ___ sullied   I. foolish acts

10. ___ sillier   J. in place of

11. ___ chillier   K. to misrepresent

12. ___ flier   L. to hold true

13. ___ collier   M. soiled

14. ___ Molière   N. loyal or faithful

15. ___ follies   O. depended on

16. ___ holier   P. aviator

17. ___ lieu   Q. Scottish dog used for herding sheep

18. ___ Joilet   R. white flowers

19. ___ relied   S. more reverent

20. ___ lieutenant   T. coal miner

21. ___ lief   U. aide or deputy

22. ___ liege   V. tools used for bending objects

Now see how many words you can think of that have the word "one" in them.

186. WORDS FROM WELL-KNOWN PEOPLE

Three quotes by famous people are hidden in this cryptogram. The author of the quote is found below the quote. Solve this cryptogram by substituting the correct letters for the letters used in the code. No letter can stand for itself. Utilize the substitution code grid below. Patience is a virtue.

1. UM OIQ RCE CZ IR IBM, NXE ZCV IWW EDAM!

NMR FCRQCR

2. D IA RCE PCXRB MRCXBU EC JRCO MTMVPEUDRB.

F.A. NIVVDM

3. WME XQ RMTMV RMBCEDIEM CXE CZ ZMIV, NXE WME XQ

RMTMV ZMIV EC RMBCEDIEM.

FCUR Z. JMRRMYP

Real letters: A B C D E F G H I J K L M N O P Q R S T U V W X Y Z

Substitute
letters: _ _ _ <u>Y</u> _ _ _ _ _ <u>F</u> _ _ _ _ <u>C</u> _ _ _ _ _ _ <u>T</u> _ _ _ _

187. "X" MARKS THE SPOT

The words below have something in common: All end with the letter x. Fill in the letters of the words that match the definitions. Then use the circled letters to identify the person who finds it important to know where "x marks the spot."

1. _ _ _ x: continual movement or change

2. _ _ x: to increase or to polish

3. _ x: a chopping tool

4. _ _ x: kiss of peace

5. _ _ ⊖⊖ _ x: whirlwind

6. _ _ x: the baseball team from Boston is the Red _____

7. _ _ _ _ x: a spiral

8. _ _ _ _ ⊖ x: a letter or letters added to a word's ending

9. ⊖ _ x: to annoy

10. ⊖ _ _ _ _ x: a letter or letters joined to the beginning of a word

11. _ ⊖ x: a sign supposed to bring bad luck

12. ⊖ _ _ x: the highest point

13. _ _ ⊖ x: to bend, as a muscle

14. _ ⊖ _ _ x: that which has been brought back or restored

15. _ ⊖ _ x: a wildcat

Bonus Answer: _ _ _ _ _ _ _   _ _ _

© 1994 by the Center for Applied Research in Education

188. THE EAR EXAM

Before you think we're heading to the doctor's office, take it easy. These twenty clues have two-word answers that rhyme with one another. Let your ears help you to solve these rhyming pair answers. Write your answers in the spaces provided. The first one is done for you.

1. <u>yellow fellow</u>   jaundiced man

2. _____ a gentle youngster

3. _____ absent female deer

4. _____ tardy Nathaniel

5. _____ house of worship tree

6. _____ huge freight-carrying boat

7. _____ an incorrect chant

8. _____ a dimmer athletic shoe

9. _____ a recent mixture of meat and vegetables

10. _____ anger on the acting platform

11. _____ an embarrased Theodore

12. _____ a boorish fop

13. _____ foolish male goat

14. _____ a dirt-splattered companion

15. _____ a chillier large rock

16. _____ a young lady from Florida's capital city

17. _____ very fat flock members

18. _____ a tremendous destiny

19. _____ half a score of Japanese coins

20. _____ Elizabeth's gas stations

189. RHYMIN' SIMON

Simon is not as simple as we may think. He has created these clues and answers to challenge you to keep up with him. Write your answers to these rhyming words in the spaces provided. The first one is done for you.

1. big rig _____ large truck

2. _____ 37th U.S. President's female foxes

3. _____ President Washington's deep narrow passages

4. _____ a rabbit's worries

5. _____ humorous rabbit

6. _____ singer Nelson's male goats

7. _____ TV talk show host Jay's shorthand writers

8. _____ explorer Lewis's friend's drug agents

9. _____ McCartney's shopping centers

10. _____ singer Joel's young female horses

11. _____ Maid of Orleans' rib cage

12. _____ 39th U.S. President's trades

13. _____ radium discoverer's angers

14. _____ basketball star Jordan's vehicles

15. _____ Marx's South American cowboys

16. _____ author Twain's sailing vessels

17. _____ news commentator Dan's soapy foam

18. _____ Hillary Clinton's husband's debts

19. _____ Gore's friends

20. _____ stories from Connecticut's Ivy League college

How many more can you create? We challenge you to make five rhyming pairs about famous people.

190. GEORGE WASHINGTON

To celebrate George Washington's birthday, answer these fifteen questions about our first U.S. President. When you have correctly answered these questions, unscramble the ten lettters found within the circles to indentify an object commonly associated with George Washington.

1. _ _ _ _ _ _ _ _ _ _ _ _ _: the war Washington fought in

2. _ _ _ _ _ _Ⓞ: the occupation of George Washington's father

3. _ _ _ _ _ _ _ _: the state of Washington's birth

4. _ _ _ _ Ⓞ _ _ _ _ _: Washington's family estate

5. _ _ _ _ Ⓞ_: Mrs. George Washington

6. _ _ _ _ _ _Ⓞ_ _ _ _ Ⓞ_ _ _ _ _ _: Washington was a member of this select group of representatives from the American colonies

7. _ _ _ _ _ _ _ _Ⓞ- _ _ - _ _ _Ⓞ_: Washington's title during the war

8. Ⓞ_ _ _ _ _ _ _: The British surrendered here

9. _ _ _ _ _ _ _ _ _ _ _ _ _: Washington's swearing in on April 20, 1789

10. _ _Ⓞ_ _: Washington's biographer

11. _ _ _ _Ⓞ_: painted Washington's portrait

12. _ _ _ _ _ : He succeeded Washington

13. _ _ _ _ _ _ _ _ _: illness that contributed to Washington's death

14. French and _ _ _ _ _ _ War: Washington also participated in this war.

15. _ _ _ _: Washington's false teeth were made of this material.

Bonus: The object associated with George Washington is the _ _ _ _ _ _ _ _ _ _.

191. OUR SIXTEENTH PRESIDENT

This month we celebrate the birth of Abraham Lincoln born in Kentucky on February 12, 1809. Identify the following sixteen words each having the letters ABE in that order within the word. Then unscramble the letters found in the circles to identify a two-word term often associated with Abe Lincoln.

1. _ A B E _ : a tag

2. _ A B E _ : a sword

3. A B _ _ _ _ _ E : positive

4. _ A B _ _ E _ : a restaurant featuring entertainment

5. _ A B _ E O : to chatter

6. _ _ A B _ E : provide with means

7. _ A B _ _ OO _ E : to make up

8. A B E _ : to encourage

9. _ O _ A B _ E : to weaken

10. _ A _ O B E _ : quality or ability

11. A B _ _ E O _ _ _ _ : to shorten

12. _ A _ B _ E : polished limestone

13. _ A B _ O E : to make incoherent sounds

14. _ _ A B _ E _ _ : dullness

15. _ _ _ A B _ _ _ _ E _ : firmly fixed

16. _ _ _ A O B E _ _ _ : red fruit

The circled letters spell _____ _____.

192. THE PRESIDENT'S RESIDENCE

This activity's title answers the question, "What is the White House?" All the answers to these questions involving U.S. Presidents are two rhyming words. Use the list of our leaders on the next page since we refer to them by what number president each was. Write the answer in the appropriate blank.

1. _____ #11's kin

2. _____ #31's windows

3. _____ #21's joker's

4. _____ #26's whirlpools

5. _____ a pale-yellow #7

6. _____ #5's enemies

7. _____ #18's insects

8. _____ #10's fashion designers

9. _____ #30's friends

10. _____ #41's shrubbery

11. _____ #42's dollars

12. _____ #33's furs

13. _____ #1's fake signatures

14. _____ #23's troops stationed in a fortified place

15. _____ #40's heathens

16. _____ #38's planks

17. _____ #39's haulers

18. _____ #19's bewilderment

19. _____ #12's chasers of large, aquatic mammals

PRESIDENTS OF THE UNITED STATES

1. George Washington
2. John Adams
3. Thomas Jefferson
4. James Madison
5. James Monroe
6. John Quincy Adams
7. Andrew Jackson
8. Martin Van Buren
9. William Henry Harrison
10. John Tyler
11. James K. Polk
12. Zachary Taylor
13. Millard Fillmore
14. Franklin Pierce
15. James Buchanan
16. Abraham Lincoln
17. Andrew Johnson
18. Ulysses S. Grant
19. Rutherford B. Hayes
20. James A. Garfield
21. Chester A. Arthur
22. Grover Cleveland
23. Benjamin Harrison
24. Grover Cleveland
25. William McKinley
26. Theodore Roosevelt
27. William Howard Taft
28. Woodrow Wilson
29. Warren G. Harding
30. Calvin Coolidge
31. Herbert Hoover
32. Franklin D. Roosevelt
33. Harry S. Truman
34. Dwight D. Eisenhower
35. John F. Kennedy
36. Lyndon B. Johnson
37. Richard M. Nixon
38. Gerald R. Ford
39. Jimmy Carter
40. Ronald Reagan
41. George Bush
42. Bill Clinton

193. WORDS HAVING MEN'S NAMES IN THEM

Twenty different men's names are given to help you identify the words defined below. Fill in the missing letters to correctly identify each one.

1. A D A M _ _ _ : unyielding

2. B E N _ _ _ _ _ _ _ : kind and charitable

3. J A C K _ _ : a short coat

4. B I L L _ _ _ _ _ : a game similar to pool

5. S T E V E _ _ _ _ : longshoreman

6. P H I L _ _ _ _ _ : the love of learning and the study of texts

7. _ L U K E : a type of fish

8. W I L L _ _ _ : done intentionally

9. E D _ _ : a whirlpool

10. M A R T I N _ _ : a strict disciplinarian

11. _ _ _ _ _ R O Y : heavy cotton fabric

12. S A L _ _ _ _ _ _ : a saving from destruction

13. _ _ B O _ : a joint in the arm

14. _ H A N K : a cut of beef from an animal's leg

15. _ _ _ D O N : a line of guards

16. _ L E E _ _ _ : happy

17. S E A N _ _ : a meeting to communicate with the dead

18. F R A N K _ _ _ _ _ _ : incense

19. K E N _ _ _ _ : an Old English poetic term denoting a name

20. _ R O N _ : a leaf

194. HIDDEN GIRLS' NAMES

The names of twenty girls are hidden within this word find. These names are contained within larger words. As an example, Amy is found within the larger word bigamy. This word has been circled for you. Circle the other nineteen words containing girls' names in this puzzle.

```
Z P G T G Y M T S E W Z B M T V M W H T F G C Y
A F G V M B J Y H B N H S P C H N S O E X L H V
D N K A T S T K B C E S N R S H H I K Q L D P Z
N I G H T I N G A L E C U F L O R I D A Y E N W
Z I K I C M D J H S S T N E H T Y I C N T O N F
B F G A N S P A H V H F G A A G F I S S I E Q A
D F R V T A S C H L C R R P R B N R W T K D P W
D E N J O Y J M E O V M E P H O V K A W I A M P
V B B Q W N J S R V B D C J M Q N R K N N A Y J
Q F M I P N S W V G A R L R S D O G X N T X N Q
M Z G B L R W Y K N H T A S T D L Q I B Z I S K
Q V N C W I G G E P G H G S A D C H D M Z X C B
R Q W W J R T R D P Y B F L L H I Q K N F N V G
Y N Q F X G E A V N Y J C W F L W S V X K N V G
Z D Y P G S D L T L V G R Z A F D R W V T J M Y
P J G Y Q Z D H P E Y S B T D W N H V W Q D B C
M Q R B W V H J T C D P E R H G R D G P D Q M Y
```

AMY	FRAN	JOY	PAT
ANN	GALE	KATE	RUTH
CHRIS	GINA	LORI	SERENA
DEB	HELEN	MONICA	SUE
DORA	IDA	NORA	VERA

195. GIRLS' NAMES IN OTHER WORDS

The twenty girls' names below all have something in common. Each has another meaning or use. As an example, June, besides being a girl's name, is also the name of the month. Match the names with their other meanings.

1. ___ CHARLOTTE   A. an herb

2. ___ LAUREL   B. a state

3. ___ HOLLY   C. the beginning of daylight

4. ___ PENNY   D. a song

5. ___ HOPE   E. beauty of form

6. ___ GINGER   F. the day before a holiday

7. ___ GALE   G. a sweet

8. ___ GRACE   H. a city in North Carolina

9. ___ GEORGIA   I. a clear, transparent quartz

10. ___ DAWN   J. a type of storm

11. ___ DALE   K. a girl, especially in Ireland

12. ___ CAROL   L. tree with pointed leaves

13. ___ COLLEEN   M. a coin

14. ___ CRYSTAL   N. economy or careful management

15. ___ FAITH   O. to want and expect

16. ___ EVE   P. trust

17. ___ PRUDENCE   Q. a family of trees or shrubs

18. ___ ROSEMARY   R. evergreen herb of the mint family

19. ___ DAISY   S. a flower

20. ___ CANDY   T. a valley

196. GET A JOB!

The last names of twenty-five famous people are hidden in this grid. Each of their last names is an occupation. Circle the hidden name and then match it with the proper first name. The first one is done for you. Discuss how each person gained his or her fame.

```
P L A Y E R P R I E S T H C W P R I N C I P A L
M O Q F G T E J E K M W A D O A B X V X X L W R
F M R K T G V K X V J W T Y G O R P M S Y H R C
Y M O T N M L S A F A Z G F L S P D G S H H S J
T O D A E B P Y G B G E H Q L O K E E P X V P N
C P R C M R K H X Q K Y W L S F R G R N M Y S T
B G V F K P K S S K C R C B J R R L K C Z B L N
R N Z T Y X L H Z M F C K J H X B V L Z D Z L R
Z R P H Q G Q B C F T J P W S S N N Z Q G T W L
Q M M B X R S R P A W V J L Q R M P M Z T C D H
Z C N S B P W S K D R T D Y O X P C D V L Z W L
M R M A X T R Z A Q S P G R T W R O W H F N J H
Y N X Q M E N R J W R I E I N C R E S X N H R D
R F G B L E C O Q X K M N N K R L I T T Z K L W
Y C R L Y H R G S Q R K X G T P B C G N M X Y V
J N E B E H V O M A E C X Q E E R D R H U A K W
F S R R E H S I F R M I L L E R R S M I T H N G
```

Anne _____   Isaac Bashevis _____   Karen _____

Carrie _____   Jack _____   Katherine Anne _____

Dennis _____   James _____   Neil _____

Fanny _____   James _____   Peter _____

Gary Player   James _____   Steve _____

George _____   James _____   Stuart _____

Governor Al _____   James Fenimore _____   Victoria _____

Grant _____   Joan _____

Holly _____   Judas _____

197. GEOFFREY WHO?

❧

This activity, featuring the names of twelve authors, will test your literary mind and ears. Authors' last names have been changed into syllables so that Geoffrey CHAUCER in this exercise is really Geoffrey to chew (chaw) + a respectful term of address for a man (sir). See how many of these authors you can identify.

1. William _____ to become unsteady + a weapon

2. Katherine _____ owned by a male + a playing area

3. John _____ opposite of down + a dam

4. John _____ a building where grain is ground + 2000 pounds

5. Emily _____ slang for a detective + opposite of out + opposite of daughter

6. _____ to frolic + one of five on the foot

7. Ernest _____ folding back and sewing down + a route

8. Laurence _____ strict

9. William _____ belonging to a group of letters + value

10. Eudora _____ a raised ridge of skin + the fifth letter of the alphabet

11. Louisa May _____ a man's name + a narrow, collapsible bed

12. Oscar _____ untamed

Name _____   Date _____   Period _____

198. HAVE A WHALE OF A TIME WITH THESE MEN

⚬⚬⚬

All these men have come to help you identify the words that fit the definitions. After you have written the correct words, the letters between the vertical lines will spell a name associated with a hint in this activity's title.

1. a pungent alcohol   M E N _|_|_ _

2. act of controlling   _ _ _ _ _ _|M E N _

3. elementary   _ _ _ _ M E N _ _ _ _|_

4. to praise   _ _ _|M E N _

5. to mourn   _ _|M E N _

6. beggar   M E N _ _ _ _ _|_

7. mirth   _ _ _ _ _|M E N _

8. mixture with water to make concrete   _ _|M E N _

9. servile   M E N _ _ _|_

10. surroundings   _ _ _ _ _ _ _|M E N _

11. salve   _ _ _ _|M E N _

12. founder of genetics   M E N _ _ _|_

13. in a short time   _ _ M E N _ _ _ _ _|_

14. cellar   _ _ _ _|M E N _

HIDDEN NAME: _ _ _ _ _ _ _ _ _ _ _ _|_ _

199. "DON'T BE SO CURT, CURT!"

Curt or Kurt, is a man's name. It also means to be brief, especially to the point of rudeness. Here are some more names, like Curt, that have other meanings associated with them. Write the name next to its meaning. The names are listed alphabetically.

1. _____ skill or craftsmanship

2. _____ a bird's beak

3. _____ to move up and down with jerky motion

4. _____ a song

5. _____ a cut of beef

6. _____ to put on a garment

7. _____ a tiny spot

8. _____ a British nobleman

9. _____ a whirlpool

10. _____ a system of religious beliefs

11. _____ candid; open; sincere

12. _____ to bully

13. _____ machine used to hitch or lift

14. _____ a thrusting weapon

15. _____ evergreen tree or shrub

16. _____ write down or record

17. _____ average or standard

18. _____ a thin line or beam of light

19. _____ to bring civil action against

20. _____ the winner

200. COMMON LAST NAMES

How familiar are you with people who share the same last name? Each of the three people in the twenty groups shares a common last name. Write the surname next to the three people.

1. _____ Bill, Ben, Omar

2. _____ Wilbur, Orville, Richard

3. _____ Bill, Hillary, De Witt

4. _____ George, Booker T., Martha

5. _____ Karl, Groucho, Harpo

6. _____ Charlotte, Emily, Anne

7. _____ Sinclair, Jerry, C.S.

8. _____ Robert E., Pinky, Harper

9. _____ Clifford, Washington, John

10. _____ Dylan, Debi, Lowell

11. _____ Teddy, Franklin, Eleanor

12. _____ Zachary, James, Lawrence

13. _____ Casey, Bobby, Quincy

14. _____ Sandra Day, Edwin, Carroll

15. _____ Tennessee, Ted, William Carlos

16. _____ Noah, Daniel, John

17. _____ August, Lanford, Willie

18. _____ Jesus, Felipe, Matty

19. _____ James, Dolly, Oscar

20. _____ Elton, Olivia Newton, Tommy

201. SPORTS CELEBRITIES

Here's your chance to display your sports knowledge. Write the sport with which each of these sixteen people is associated. Score one point for each correct answer.

ACROSS CLUES

2. Joe Namath
8. Chris Evert
9. Mark Spitz
10. Hulk Hogan
13. Carl Lewis
14. Arnold Palmer
15. Pele
16. Ted Turner

DOWN CLUES

1. Wayne Gretzky
3. Nolan Ryan
4. Muhammad Ali
5. Mary Lou Retton
6. Michael Jordan
7. Greta Weitz
11. Eddie Arcaro
12. Prince Charles

Answer Keys

The Roots and Limbs of Our Language

Word Games 1–26

1. ROOTS AND PREFIXES

1.	J	9.	H
2.	A	10.	F
3.	C	11.	I
4.	K	12.	G
5.	L	13.	D
6.	E	14.	O
7.	N	15.	M
8.	B		

The men's names are: Jack, Len, and Dom. The fruit is the fig. The U.S. President's initials are B.H. (Benjamin Harrison).

2. "ROOT"INELY MATCHING UP THE WORDS

1.	S (spirit)	9.	R (all)
2.	T (mankind)	10.	E (love)
3.	A	11.	N (after)
4.	R (short)	12.	G
5.	T (trust)	13.	I
6.	Y	14.	N (sleep)
7.	O	15.	E (to turn)
8.	U	16.	S (to conquer)

What are the Indianapolis 500 drivers told on Memorial Day? "Start your engines!"

3. PREFIX WORD FIND

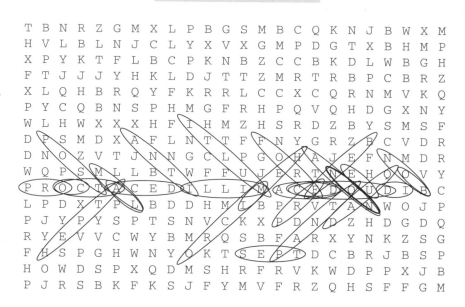

```
T  B  N  R  Z  G  M  X  L  P  B  G  S  M  B  C  Q  K  N  J  B  W  X  M
H  V  L  B  L  N  J  C  L  Y  X  V  X  G  M  P  D  G  T  X  B  H  M  P
X  P  Y  K  T  F  L  B  C  P  K  N  B  Z  C  C  B  K  D  L  W  B  G  H
F  T  J  J  J  Y  H  K  L  D  J  T  T  Z  M  R  T  R  B  P  C  B  R  Z
X  L  Q  H  B  R  Q  Y  F  K  R  R  L  C  C  X  C  Q  R  N  M  V  K  Q
P  Y  C  Q  B  N  S  P  H  M  G  F  R  H  P  Q  V  Q  H  D  G  X  N  Y
W  L  H  W  X  X  X  H  F  I  H  M  Z  H  S  R  D  Z  B  Y  S  M  S  F
D  P  S  M  D  X  A  F  L  N  T  T  F  N  Y  G  R  Z  B  C  V  D  R
D  N  O  Z  V  T  J  N  G  C  L  P  G  O  H  A  J  E  F  N  M  D  R
W  Q  P  S  M  L  L  B  T  W  F  F  U  J  E  R  T  N  E  H  Q  V  Y
P  R  O  C  U  A  C  E  D  I  L  L  I  M  A  C  E  D  O  U  D  I  B  C
L  P  D  X  T  P  L  B  D  D  H  M  I  B  P  R  V  T  A  N  W  O  J  P
P  J  Y  P  Y  S  P  T  S  N  V  C  K  X  P  D  N  D  Z  H  D  G  D  Q
R  Y  E  V  V  C  W  Y  B  M  R  Q  S  B  F  A  R  X  Y  N  K  Z  S  G
F  H  S  P  G  H  W  N  Y  O  K  T  S  E  P  T  D  C  B  R  J  B  S  P
H  O  W  D  S  P  X  Q  D  M  S  H  R  F  R  V  K  W  D  P  P  X  J  B
P  J  R  S  B  K  F  K  S  J  F  Y  M  V  F  R  Z  Q  H  S  F  F  G  M
```

Here are the prefixes next to their meanings:

after-post	*eight-oct, octa*	*half-hemi*	*ten-dec, deca*
against-anti	*entire-panto*	*many-multi*	*thousand-milli*
against-ob	*for-pro*	*nine-nona*	*twelve-duodec*
against-oc	*four-quad*	*not-non*	*two-bi, di*
bad-mal	*good-bene*	*seven-hepta*	
before-fore	*good-bon*	*seven-sept*	
before-pre	*good-eu*	*small-micro*	

4. THE POWER OF PREFIXES

1. antidote
2. antecedent
3. bellicose
4. converse
5. submarine
6. contravene
7. review
8. intramurals
9. intermediate
10. paradox
11. perimeter
12. miniscule
13. euphony
14. misgivings
15. premeditate
16. nonsense
17. ultrasound
18. hypochondriac
19. biography
20. expand

The famous women in U.S. history are (SUSAN B.) ANTHONY and (FLORENCE) NIGHTINGALE.

5. PICKING AND CHOOSING WORD PARTS

1. omnipotent
2. benediction
3. misanthrope
4. polyglot
5. macrodont
6. annual
7. neophyte
8. apoplexy

9. hyperbole
10. biostatics
11. demagogue
12. pedantry
13. hypodermic
14. philatelist
15. maladroit

6. A HOST OF ROOTS AND PREFIXES

1. E.
2. O
3. N
4. P
5. C
6. B
7. G
8. F
9. D
10. S

11. A
12. T
13. H
14. K
15. M
16. L
17. J
18. R
19. I
20. Q

Quote: All modern American literature comes from one book by Mark Twain called *Huckleberry Finn.* American writing comes from that. (Hemingway)

7. DIGGING UP THE ROOTS

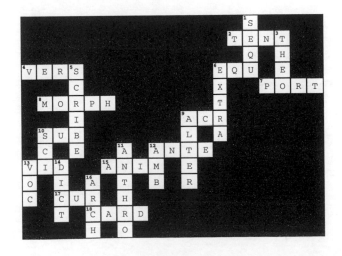

8. BUILDING WORDS

1. paradoxical
2. eugenics
3. incumbancy
4. congregation
5. recognize
6. enumerate
7. affirmative
8. intravenous
9. different
10. manufacture
11. aggression
12. digested
13. impediment

9. IT'S ALL IN THE NUMBERS

1. 4
2. 8
3. 16
4. 32
5. 64
6. 128
7. 256
8. 512
9. 1024
10. 2048

Bonus: Each number is double the one before it.

10. AVOIDING TWITDOM!

1. k
2. f
3. b
4. c
5. g
6. h
7. d
8. m
9. e
10. l
11. n
12. i
13. j
14. o
15. a

11. I SAY OLD CHAP!

1.	c	10.	i
2.	f	11.	r
3.	g	12.	n
4.	q	13.	o
5.	h	14.	k
6.	j	15.	p
7.	d	16.	m
8.	b	17.	e
9.	a	18.	l

The five letter British term for infant is *bairn* (#'s 8–12).

12. SOME GIFTS FROM THE FRENCH

1.	F	10.	G
2.	Q	11.	J
3.	E	12.	D
4.	L	13.	C
5.	K	14.	N
6.	M	15.	I
7.	H	16.	O
8.	A	17.	B
9.	P		

13. ARE YOU WISE TO EDELWEISS?

1.	L	9.	A
2.	M	10.	D
3.	P	11.	J
4.	I	12.	N
5.	O	13.	H
6.	F	14.	K
7.	G	15.	B
8.	C	16.	E

14. CAN A BAMBINO TAKE A GONDOLA INTO THE BLUE GROTTO?

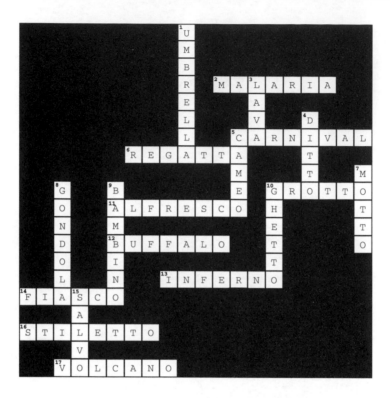

15. ITALIAN FOODS AND DRINKS

16. LATIN WORDS AND PHRASES

1.	f	11.	g
2.	h	12.	q
3.	m	13.	o
4.	k	14.	b
5.	d	15.	i
6.	p	16.	a
7.	e	17.	s
8.	c	18.	r
9.	l	19.	t
10.	n	20.	j

17. OWSDR MORF HET PSHSINA

1.	COCKROACH	9.	POTATO
2.	TOMATO	10.	GAUCHO
3.	TUNA	11.	CACAO
4.	BARRACUDA	12.	MARIJUANA
5.	MOSQUITO	13.	BANANA
6.	CANOE	14.	COCONUT
7.	TORNADO	15.	PONCHO
8.	CIGAR	16.	BARBEQUE

18. TELL ME WHERE YOU'RE FROM!

1.	Q	10.	H
2.	D	11.	N
3.	B	12.	I
4.	M	13.	A
5.	P	14.	O
6.	J	15.	G
7.	F	16.	C
8.	K	17.	E
9.	L		

19. DO AS THE ROMANS DO

1. J
2. K
3. I
4. O
5. B
6. E
7. C
8. P
9. S
10. D

11. G
12. N
13. F
14. R
15. H
16. T
17. L
18. M
19. Q
20. A

20. CRAZY EIGHTS

1. communal
2. decorate
3. educated
4. extender

5. handsome
6. positive
7. romantic
8. sullenly

21. GRAB BAG

1. bracelet
2. cutup
3. dependable
4. doctorate
5. feather
6. goodbye
7. grimace
8. handkerchief
9. hardtack
10. heart

11. justice
12. kneecap
13. lipstick
14. looseleaf
15. margin
16. necklace
17. partridge
18. patronage
19. streetcar
20. throughway

Bonus: Some states that are compound words are: Colorado, Indiana, and Washington. Some states that have three words in them are: Colorado, Connecticut, Missouri, Ohio, Virginia. States with four are: Illinois, Louisiana, Mississippi, North Carolina, and South Carolina.

22. NOUNS SHARING THE SAME ADJECTIVE

1. dry
2. golden
3. right
4. big
5. close or tight
6. light
7. wet
8. lost
9. red
10. bad

11. white
12. ice
13. old
14. sweet
15. flying
16. dark
17. letter
18. silver
19. green

23. ODDS AND EVENS

Possible answers include:

A. assuage, awoke, cagey, comes, goose, kiosk, macaw, magic, moose, mouse, music, quick, smack

B. ballet, defer, delude, denude, feline, fodder, pedal, riddle, tater

C. afghan, cheery, glory, glove, opera, snare, stare, stuff, wrench

24. A SCORE OF WORDS

Here are some possible answers (in alphabetical order) to the word *WONDERFUL:*
done, down, drew, endow, fend, flow, flower, found, frond, frown, fund, lure, nerd, node, redo, round, rude, under, wonder, word

Here are some possible answers (in alphabetical order) to the word *SWITZERLAND:*
darn, dent, earl, elan, land, rail, rale, rend, rile, seal, seat, swan, swirl, tend, tern, trail, trial, trend, wand, wind

Here are some possible answers (in alphabetical order) to the word *SANDERS:*
Andes, Dane, dare, dean, dear, dress, earn, nard, near, nerd, read, rend, resand, sand, sane, saner, sedan, send, sends, snare

25. HOW A GREENHOUSE BECAME A TINSMITH

Answers will vary.

26. WE NEED AL!

1. RE...cadre, report, bread
2. LO...reload, locater, loan
3. ET...billet, petal, mallet
4. SO...sorely, solid, soother
5. OW...coward, lowest, cowlick
6. BE...become, lobe, beat

7. AN... bean, anthem, manage
8. WO...swoon, woman, woken
9. HE...theater, cheap, heart
10. ED...pedal, federal, redeal
11. TH...throw, teeth, hearth
12. CL...clone, clink, clash
13. EL...fellow, elbow, delude

The Tools of Communication

Word Games 27–55

27. MATCH THEM WITH THEIR MATES

1.	abbess	11.	heroine
2.	aviatrix	12.	queen
3.	baroness	13.	lassie
4.	nanny goat	14.	lady
5.	sow	15.	matriarch
6.	cow	16.	ewe
7.	filly	17.	hen
8.	duchess	18.	tigress
9.	countess	19.	tsarine
10.	empress	20.	usherette

28. "…LEND ME YOUR EARS"

1.	B, Q	11.	P, A
2.	A, C	12.	L, G
3.	M, K	13.	N, M
4.	E, B	14.	O, H
5.	R, E	15.	J, J
6.	H, D	16.	D, I
7.	G, L	17.	C, R
8.	I, O	18.	Q, S
9.	F, F	19.	K, N
10.	S, T	20.	T, P

29. BREAK A LEG!

1. neck
2. arm, leg
3. lip
4. hand
5. lip
6. knee
7. ear
8. head
9. back
10. foot

11. vein
12. back
13. nose
14. heart
15. toe
16. toe
17. eye
18. skull
19. thumb
20. eye, eye
21. heel

30. THE COLORFUL WORLD OF WORDS

1. blue
2. red
3. yellow
4. black
5. white
6. silver
7. brown
8. green
9. black, blue
10. red
11. red
12. black

13. red
14. gray
15. blue
16. yellow
17. black
18. red
19. white
20. blue
21. green
22. gray
23. blue
24. blue
25. black

31. IS THIS YOUR ACHILLES' HEEL?

1. heel
2. below
3. change
4. dead
5. elbow

11. caboodle
12. line
13. now
14. wagon
15. pen

6. fifth
7. greek
8. high
9. bliss
10. jump

16. mouse
17. revenge
18. turkey
19. vanish
20. deal

The woman whose beauty was the cause of the Trojan War was *Helen of Troy*.

32. PALINDROMES

1. radar
2. level
3. madam
4. peep
5. bob
6. deed
7. toot
8. noon
9. boob
10. poop
11. rotor

12. redder
13. solos
14. refer
15. civic
16. stats
17. tenet
18. shahs
19. sagas
20. kayak
21. eye

Phrase: Star Comedy by Democrats

33. UNSCRAMBLING PROVERBS

1. Only the good die young.
2. Boys will be boys.
3. Don't cry over spilled milk.
4. Look before you leap.
5. Seeing is believing.
6. Still waters run deep.
7. Don't look a gift horse in the mouth.
8. The squeaky wheel gets the oil.
9. Only the strong survive.
10. A chain is as strong as its weakest link.
11. Absence makes the heart grow fonder.

34. PROVERBS

1. pot
2. hesitates
3. wins
4. company
5. Actions
6. angels
7. twice
8. fool
9. best
10. hurt
11. divided
12. stones
13. Cleanliness
14. safe
15. name
16. rope
17. sufficient
18. woman's

35. DOUBLESPEAK

1. r
2. d
3. c
4. o
5. b
6. i
7. h
8. a
9. g
10. n
11. p
12. s
13. m
14. l
15. f
16. t
17. q
18. e
19. j
20. k

36. MORE DOUBLESPEAK

1. plutonium contamination
2. blackmail payments
3. truck's mud flaps
4. nuclear warhead
5. flashlight
6. nuclear reactor fire
7. lies
8. neutron bomb
9. killing
10. wellness
11. remedial courses
12. war
13. girdle
14. chicken coop
15. military retreat

37. AS EASY AS PIE!

1. rain
2. fiddle
3. dozen
4. x
5. light
6. behind
7. old
8. highway
9. quick
10. ifs
11. toe
12. April
13. mad
14. under
15. cold

38. HAVE YOU MET MY BETTER HALF?

1. e
2. m
3. g
4. n
5. q
6. r
7. a
8. c
9. o
10. l
11. d
12. f
13. i
14. s
15. h
16. j
17. b
18. p
19. t
20. k

The hidden cliché is *cold fish* (#'s 8–15).

39. CLEO, QUEEN OF THE CLICHÉS

line...cliché
1. as cold as ice
2. flat as a pancake, blanket of snow
3. as smooth as glass, silhouetted against the sky
4. patter of rain
5. raining cats and dogs, ocean's roar
6. pretty as a picture, God's country

7. crack of dawn, black as coal, ominous silence
8. looms on the horizon
9. as fresh as a daisy, stand like sentinels
10. little by little, all its glory
11. as white as snow
12. life of Riley

40. THE NEWS REPORTS: HANK SMITH LEADS A DOG'S LIFE

1. horse
2. apple
3. lion
4. clam
5. cheese
6. pancake
7. nuts
8. skunk

9. peas
10. beaver
11. bird
12. egg
13. pie
14. fox
15. dog
16. duck

41. HOW AM I SUPPOSED TO TAKE THAT?

1. man
2. brand
3. low
4. gnome
5. mouse
6. cleave
7. court
8. peer
9. belt
10. peep

11. purse
12. object
13. stage
14. defect
15. pelt
16. draft
17. spat
18. hawk
19. foot
20. spare

The two bonus words are RUN and SET.

42. WORDS WITH MULTIPLE MEANINGS

The following are possible answers:

1. *call:* already done on activity page
2. *fast:* not easily moved; swift; abstaining from food; living a rich lifestyle

3. *fret:* to eat away; to worry; lateral ridge on a guitar; ornamental architectural relief

4. *sack:* bag; dismissal from employment; to tackle a quarterback; to plunder or loot

5. *strike:* hit; to announce time; afflict with disease; in baseball, a pitch in certain zone

6. *run:* to go by moving the legs rapidly; melt and flow; to be in charge of; be a candidate for election

7. *band:* a wedding ring; group of musicians; to untie for a common purpose; narrow strip of cloth

8. *beat:* strike; whip; defeat; cheat

9. *brace:* tie firmly; prop up; device that clasps; device to straighten teeth

10. *break:* cause to come apart; tame with force; exchange a bill for coins; opening shot in a billiards game

43. THE LAST SHALL BE FIRST AND THE FIRST SHALL BE LAST

1. oleo	12. gang
2. lentil	13. wallow
3. Israeli	14. blurb
4. sass	15. elegance
5. dread	16. nylon
6. kayak	17. plump
7. caustic	18. tenet
8. fief	19. ulu
9. yesterday	20. railler
10. anemia	21. momentum
11. high	

44. NO IF'S, AND'S, OR BUT'S . . .

1. a*but*	11. l*if*e
2. *but*ter	12. m*and*ate
3. comm*and*	13. ni*ft*y
4. de*but*	14. offh*and*
5. err*and*	15. p*and*a
6. fals*ify*	16. qu*and*ary
7. gr*and*	17. s*and*al
8. hali*but*	18. tr*if*le
9. isl*and*	19. upl*if*t
10. j*iff*y	20. wh*iff*

45. "CPTN! M CPTN!"

1. chief
2. head
3. leader
4. boss
5. foreman
6. superior
7. overseer
8. manager

9. dean
10. master
11. motivator
12. director
13. conductor
14. supervisor
15. principal
16. commander
17. superintendent

46. THE DENTS THAT COST

1. trident
2. indent
3. Occident
4. dental
5. rodent
6. prudent
7. student
8. evident
9. accident

10. denture
11. providential
12. resident
13. incident
14. transcendental
15. indenture
16. president
17. dentist
18. precedent

"I do not understand it!"

47. GOLLY GEE! THE G'S HAVE GOT IT!

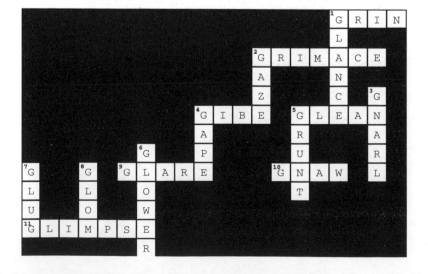

48. DOUBLE YOUR PLEASURE

a.	bazaar	m.	hammer
b.	quibble	n.	innate
c.	moccasin	o.	poodle
d.	coddle	p.	happiness
e.	eerie	r.	sorry
f.	baffle	s.	sassy
g.	haggle	t.	belittle
h.	myrhh	u.	vacuum
i.	radii	v.	savvy
k.	Hanukkah	x.	Exxon
l.	idyll	z.	dizzy

49. DROP THAT LETTER RIGHT NOW!

1.	wilder, wider	8.	label, Abel
2.	sling, sing	9.	wilt, wit
3.	plower, power	10.	bland, band
4.	slow, sow	11.	glee, gee
5.	growl, grow	12.	slate, sate
6.	play, pay	13.	clan, can
7.	least, east	14.	shell, hell
		15.	blower, lower

50. I'LL DRINK TO THAT!

1.	D	11.	B
2.	J	12.	L
3.	K	13.	H
4.	A	14.	S
5.	Q	15.	C
6.	I	16.	M
7.	R	17.	G
8.	P	18.	T
9.	O	19.	N
10.	E	20.	F

The famous hidden author is POE (#'s 8–10).

51. HOW PROUD!

The other words found in the grid are: cocky, content, glad, pleased, and satisfied.

52. WORDS WORTH THEIR WEIGHT IN GOLD

1.	caught	14.	august
2.	laud	15.	jaunty
3.	daughter	16.	augury
4.	daub	17.	gaudy
5.	hautboy	18.	auction
6.	aura	19.	naughty
7.	auk	20.	bauxite
8.	augment	21.	applause
9.	taut	22.	rondeau
10.	audience	23.	tableau
11.	paucity	24.	beau
12.	raucous	25.	bureau
13.	austere		

53. LUCKY SEVEN'S

Puzzle 1
```
s c a l d e d
c   m   e   e
h   o   s   f
e   e   p   u
m   b   i   n
e   a   s   c
r e s p e c t
```

Puzzle 2
```
b r o c a d e
l   m   l   m
e   i   l   b
s   n   e   a
s   o   g   s
e   u   e   s
d e s t r o y
```

54. SILENT FIRST LETTERS

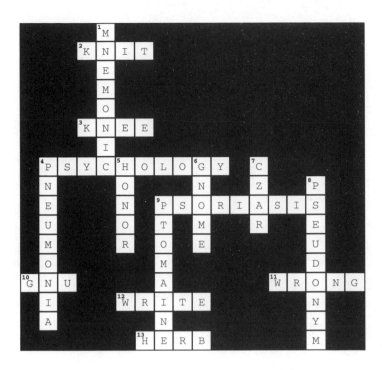

55. YOU WILL START IT... U WILL END IT

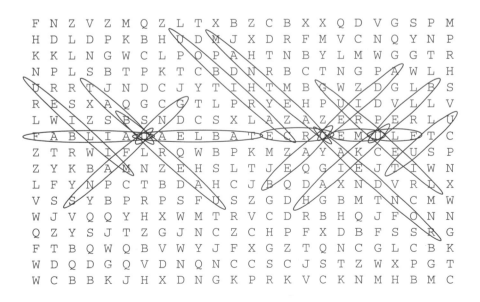

1.	*haiku*	Japanese style of poetry
2.	*bleu*	a type of cheese
3.	*ecru*	beige
4.	*manteau*	cloak
5.	*flu*	colloquial for a virus
6.	*bureau*	dresser
7.	*adieu*	goodbye
8.	*gnu*	large African antelope
9.	*caribou*	large North American reindeer
10.	*emu*	large flightless bird
11.	*snafu*	mishap
12.	*lieu*	place; stead
13.	*tabu*	sacred prohibition
14.	*tutu*	short ballet apparel
15.	*fabliau*	short story in verse
16.	*rondeau*	short, lyrical poem
17.	*milieu*	social or cultural setting
18.	*guru*	spiritual advisor
19.	*tableau*	striking dramatic scene
20.	*beau*	suitor

The World Around You

Word Games 56–92

56. THE HUMAN BODY

1. heel
2. tooth
3. shin
4. hip
5. arm
6. knee
7. chin
8. toe
9. ear
10. leg

11. lip
12. head
13. face
14. liver
15. neck
16. hand
17. knuckle
18. mouth
19. ankle
20. rib

The three other body parts found in the circled letters are:
T O N G U E   N O S E   B A C K

57. BODY PARTS WORD MAZE

1. LEG
2. TOE
3. ANKLE
4. JAW
5. HEART
6. NOSE

7. EYE
8. HEAD
9. KNEE
10. EAR
11. GUM
12. HEEL
13. NECK

58. WORDS YOU CAN TASTE

Here are suggested answers for the questions. Other foods may fit the blank.

1.	apple	14.	olive
2.	pear	15.	grapefruit
3.	Orange	16.	peanut, shrimp, munchkin
4.	cauliflower	17.	meatball, turkey, banana
5.	lemon	18.	cabbage, lettuce, dough, beans
6.	plum	19.	hot-dog
7.	Raisin	20.	chicken
8.	prune, lemon	21.	string bean
9.	squash, jam	22.	peach
10.	banana	23.	tomato
11.	corn	24.	jam, pickle
12.	date	25.	lamb
13.	carrot		

59. WORDS GOOD ENOUGH TO EAT

Possible answers are:

1.	meat	8.	pea
2.	egg	9.	corn
3.	yam	10.	candy
4.	pear	11.	steak
5.	jam	12.	stew
6.	jelly	13.	apple
7.	date		

60. MATCH THEIR MATES

1.	she-bear	11.	goose
2.	queen	12.	mare
3.	cow	13.	lioness
4.	hen	14.	female
5.	doe	15.	doe
6.	jenny	16.	ewe
7.	duck	17.	pen

8. cow
9. vixen
10. nanny

18. sow
19. tigress
20. cow

61. FERRET OUT THESE ANSWERS!

1. j
2. k
3. b
4. d
5. f
6. n
7. r
8. i
9. o
10. q

11. s
12. p
13. m
14. h
15. l
16. a
17. c
18. e
19. t
20. g

62. A BAND OF GORILLAS

1. covey
2. leap
3. skulk
4. yoke
5. band
6. exaltation
7. herd
8. pride
9. school
10. bed

11. troop
12. swarm
13. tribe
14. flock
15. gaggle
16. colony
17. watch
18. pod
19. pack
20. litter

63. FOR THE BIRDS

1. hawk
2. crane
3. auk
4. canary
5. catbird

23. tern
24. partridge
25. sparrow
26. wren
27. oriole

6.	nightingale	28.	avocet
7.	eagle	29.	turkey
8.	cardinal	30.	stork
9.	owl	31.	coot
10.	lark	32.	blackbird
11.	bluebird	33.	robin
12.	woodpecker	34.	chickadee
13.	woodcock	35.	parrot
14.	crow	36.	pigeon
15.	lovebird	37.	loon
16.	falcon	38.	vulture
17.	emu	39.	swallow
18.	quail	40.	sandpiper
19.	gull	41.	hummingbird
20.	whippoorwill	42.	mockingbird
21.	starling	43.	ostrich
22.	nighthawk	44.	chimney swift

64. THE PARADE OF INSTRUMENTS

1.	bassoon W	9.	oboe W
2.	clarinet W	10.	violin S
3.	French horn W	11.	cello S
4.	English horn W	12.	bass S
5.	drums P	13.	xylophone P
6.	bass clarinet W	14.	cymbals P
7.	flute W	15.	triangle P
8.	piccolo W	16.	trombone B
		17.	sousaphone B

65. A WORLD OF NATIONS

1.	French	14.	German
2.	Dane	15.	India
3.	American	16.	Chinese
4.	Dutch	17.	Polish
5.	English	18.	Spanish

6. Brazil
7. Irish
8. Portuguese
9. Canadian
10. Belgian
11. Hungarian
12. Russian
13. Swiss or American

19. Swedish or Italian
20. Italian or French
21. Persian
22. Irish
23. Grecian
24. Japanese
25. Turkish or Roman
26. Columbian or Irish
27. French

66. THE ROADS THAT ARE TAKEN

1. turnpike
2. highway
3. rotary
4. lane
5. street
6. bypass
7. court
8. boulevard
9. drive
10. artery

11. parkway
12. expressway
13. route
14. avenue
15. thruway
16. service road
17. causeway
18. freeway
19. thoroughfare

The answer key to the letters is:

Real letters: A B C D E F G H I J K L M N O P Q R S T U V W X Y Z
Substitute letters: Y E A T Z N R S C M X F B L H Q G D K V P W U I J O

67. PLACES IN NAMES

1. London (England)
2. Jordan (country)
3. Georgia (state)
4. France (country)
5. Montana (state)
6. Denver (CO)
7. Houston (TX)
8. Jackson (MS)
9. Cleveland (OH)

13. Charlotte (NC)
14. Raleigh (NC)
15. Olympia (WA)
16. Pierre (SD)
17. Madison (WI)
18. Lawrence (MA or KS)
19. Milton (PA or MA)
20. Mansfield (OH)
21. Whittier (CA)

10. Springfield (MA or MS)
11. Orlando (FL)
12. Washington (state)

22. Eugene (OR)
23. Manchester (NH)
24. Lowell (MA)
25. Fairbanks (AK)

68. THE STATES' ABBREVIATIONS *(PART ONE)*

1. calorie, Alabama
2. rake, Alaska
3. azure, Arizona
4. barter, Arkansas
5. catastrophe, California
6. cobalt, Colorado
7. succinct, Connecticut
8. detail, Delaware
9. flour, Florida
10. gaze, Georgia
11. chirp, Hawaii
12. riddle, Idaho

13. filter, Illinois
14. indigo, Indiana
15. giant, Iowa
16. kickstand, Kansas
17. murky, Kentucky
18. plague, Louisiana
19. scheme, Maine
20. Omdurman, Maryland
21. smash, Massachusetts
22. diminish, Michigan
23. damn, Minnesota
24. trams, Mississippi

69. THE STATES' ABBREVIATIONS *(PART TWO)*

1. momentum, Missouri
2. Amtrak, Montana
3. kneel, Nebraska
4. invade, Nevada
5. inhale, New Hampshire
6. injure, New Jersey
7. inmate, New Mexico
8. ebony, New York
9. inch, North Carolina
10. endeavor, North Dakota
11. cohesive, Ohio
12. token, Oklahoma

13. portion, Oregon
14. spatial, Pennsylvania
15. ridicule, Rhode Island
16. mischief, South Carolina
17. misdirect, South Dakota
18. smartness, Tennessee
19. mutton, Utah
20. govt., Vermont
21. vaccine, Virginia
22. waif, Wahington
23. wish, Wisconsin
24. snowy, Wyoming

70. LITTLE VENICE IN SOUTH AMERICA

1.	e	11.	d
2.	k	12.	b
3.	n	13.	s
4.	p	14.	m
5.	a	15.	f
6.	g	16.	i
7.	t	17.	l
8.	c	18.	o
9.	r	19.	j
10.	q	20.	h

71. THE SPORTING LIFE

1.	j	11.	c
2.	n	12.	m
3.	g	13.	f
4.	a	14.	d
5.	l	15.	k
6.	q	16.	s
7.	t	17.	o
8.	e	18.	r
9.	b	19.	p
10.	h	20.	i

The SPORT OF KINGS IS *HORSE RACING*.

72. A TREE IS A TREE IS A TREE?

1.	H	asp	10.	R	time
2.	C	ashen	11.	A	tango
3.	N	leech	12.	L	oar
4.	I	birth	13.	M	calm

5.	B	cheery	14.	K	pint
6.	O	toffee	15.	Q	glum
7.	F	late	16.	E	peak
8.	P	elf	17.	D	pillow
9.	G	folly	18.	J	few

73. THE FOUR MATH OPERATIONS

74. THE WORLD OF MATHEMATICS

1.	triangle	7.	angle
2.	quotient	8.	symmetry
3.	circles	9.	ratio
4.	radius	10.	addition
5.	number	11.	arithmetic
6.	geometry	12.	hypotenuse

The two math terms are *algebra* and *calculus.*

75. A NUMBER OF THINGS

1. 365-1/4 days in a year
2. 50 United States States
3. 4 quarts in a gallon
4. 10 pennies in a dime
5. 7 Wonders of the Ancient World
6. 101 dalmatians
7. 30 days hath September
8. 4 seasons in a year
9. 1001 Arabian Nights
10. 435 members of the House of Representatives
11. 7 oceans of the world
12. 3 blind mice (see how they run)
13. 95 theses of Martin Luther
14. 1492 the year Columbus sailed the ocean blue
15. 10 dimes in a dollar
16. 3 feet in a yard
17. 10 kilometers in 6.2 miles
18. 5280 feet in a mile
19. 8 parts of speech
20. 88 keys on a piano

76. LAND FORMATIONS

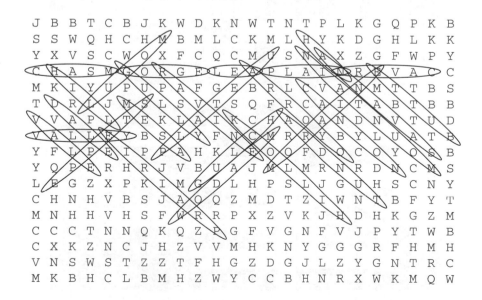

77. IT'S ELEMENTARY, MY DEAR WATSON

1. FEAR...iron (FE) + argon (AR)
2. CRAG...chromium (CR + silver (AG)
3. PANE...protactinium (PA) + neon (NE)
4. CLONE...chlorine (CL) + oxygen (O) + neon (NE)
5. BEER...beryllium (BE) + erbium (ER)
6. GAIN...gallium (GA) + iodine (I) + nitrogen (N)
7. NEAR...neon (NE) + argon (AR)
8. CUTE...copper (CU) + tellurium (TE)
9. GAS...gallium (GA) + sulphur (S)
10. BROTH...bromine (BR) + oxygen (O) + thorium (TH)
11. COAL...cobalt (CO) + aluminum (AL)
12. SICK...silicon (SI) + carbon (C) + potassium (K)
13. BIAS...bismuth (BI) + arsenic (AS)
14. LUCK...lutetium (LU) + carbon (C) + potassium (K)
15. XENOPHOBE...xenon (XE) + nitrogen (N) + oxygen (O) + phosphorous (P) + hydrogen (H) + oxygen (O) + beryllium (BE)

78. IT'S ALL IN THE STARS!

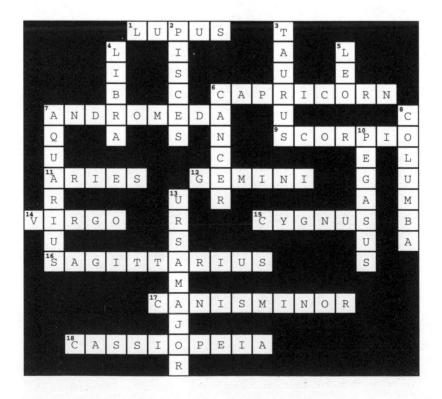

79. SIZING UP YOU SCIENCE SENSE

80. A MEATY ISSUE

1. DUCK
2. ROAST BEEF
3. STEAK
4. SAUSAGE
5. LAMB
6. TURKEY
7. CHICKEN
8. BACON

9. LIVER
10. FILET MIGNON
11. VEAL
12. HOT DOG
13. FRESH HAM
14. HAM
15. PORK
16. VENISON
17. TENDERLOIN

Letter: A B C D E F G H I J K L M N O P Q R S T U V W X Y Z

Substitute: A B C D E F G H I J K L M N O P Q R S T U V W X Y Z

81. THE PRESIDENTS' ROUNDUP

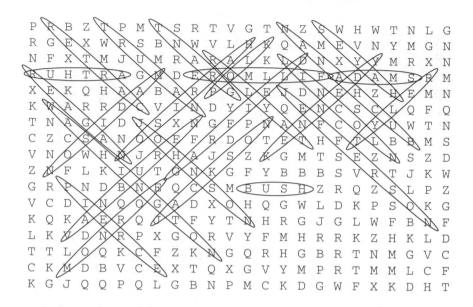

John Adams	*Andrew* (or *Lyndon*) Johnson
Chester Arthur	*John* Kennedy
James Buchanan	*Abraham* Lincoln
George Bush	*James* Madison
Jimmy Carter	*James* Monroe
Millard Fillmore	*Franklin* Pierce
James Garfield	*James* Polk
Ulysses Grant	*Ronald* Reagan
William (or *Benjamin*)	*Zachary* Taylor
Harrison	*Harry* Truman
Rutherford Hayes	*John* Tyler
Andrew Jackson	*Martin* Van Buren
Thomas Jefferson	*George* Washington

82. THE UNITED STATES

1. Alaska
2. Michigan
3. South Carolina

11. Alabama
12. Delaware
13. Kentucky

4. Oregon
5. Wisconsin
6. California
7. New Jersey
8. Nebraska
9. Montana
10. Illinois

14. Florida
15. New York
16. Oklahoma
17. Colorado
18. Texas
19. Louisiana
20. Maryland

The four state are: Idaho, Iowa, Kansas, and Maine.

83. U.S. PRESIDENTS

1. Garfield
2. Polk
3. Adams
4. Truman
5. Grant
6. Hayes
7. Filmore
8. Carter
9. Bush
10. Reagan

11. Tyler
12. Coolidge
13. Pierce
14. Harrison
15. Ford
16. Harding
17. Wilson
18. Cleveland
19. Kennedy

Bonus: The presidents' names that end with "-son" are: Jefferson, Madison, Jackson, Harrison, and Johnson.

84. A CAPITAL TRIP

1. N
2. Y
3. Y
4. Y
5. Y
6. Y
7. Y

8. N
9. N
10. Y
11. Y
12. Y
13. N
14. Y
15. N

85. WHERE AM I?

1. Chicago
2. Philadelphia
3. Indianapolis
4. Santa Fe
5. Gettysburg
6. Montgomery
7. Milwaukee
8. Boston
9. Annapolis
10. Washington, DC
11. New York City
12. Raleigh
13. Saint Augustine
14. Los Angeles
15. New Orleans
16. Oklahoma City
17. Honolulu
18. Colorado Springs

86. RHYMING WITH HISTORICAL FIGURES

1. Allen's gallons
2. Bloomer's rumors
3. De Gaulle's malls
4. Freud's voids
5. Key's seas
6. King's rings
7. Magellan's melons
8. Mann's pans
9. Moses' roses
10. Porter's orders
11. Rogers' dodgers
12. Salk's talks
13. Skinner's thinners
14. Stowe's woes
15. Wren's pens
16. Young's lungs

87. THE IN CROWD

1. league
2. inaugurate
3. quake
4. unequivocal
5. interlude
6. dupe
7. apropos
8. threaten
9. envelop
10. defeat
11. artless
12. link
13. loyal

The man who completely settled his debts *liquidated all.*

88. YOU ARE A PART OF ME

1. letter
2. cave
3. flower
4. White House
5. baseball field
6. dollar bill
7. Jewish ritual items
8. car parts
9. courtroom
10. sailboat
11. tooth
12. woodburning stove
13. newspaper's page
14. fire engine
15. circus

89. THE ODD-MAN OUT

GROUP'S NAME	ODD-MAN OUT
1. drinks	elegiac
2. Irish playwrights	Rawlings
3. cakes	nectarine
4. ways to join things	elegant
5. musical instruments	shaft
6. leaders	tattoo
7. errors	halcyon
8. denunciations	eulogy
9. rooms	myopic
10. characters from *A Tale of Two Cities*	Iago
11. cheeses	nebulous
12. sciences	gastric
13. coats	wicker
14. items worn on the head	ascot
15. types of fish	yelp

The hidden name is ERNEST HEMINGWAY.

90. WHAT DO WE HAVE IN COMMON?

1. Bridges
2. Magazines
3. Three Musketeers
4. Coins
5. Books by Judy Blume
6. Explorers
7. Wars

8. Broadway plays
9. Names for Chicago
10. Capes
11. Triangles
12. Mounts (mountains)
13. U.S. Capital Cities
14. Eponyms
15. Words from India

91. FOLLOW THE LETTER WORD GRID

										E							
	X			M						D		L	I	A	T	E	D
	Y		L					A	I								
	L		A				M		R								
	O	B	B			N			T								
	P			S					S								
E	H				E												A
F	O				P	N	A	R	D	N	U	T				R	
F	N			U			T				S				E		
I	E		C								O		P				
G			C								H	O					
Y		I		N	O	V	I	C	E		G						
	H																
										E	K	I	D	N	O	L	K

a. *ab*sent
b. *det*ail
c. *eff*igy
d. *gh*ost
e. *hic*cup
f. *Kl*ondike
g. ba*lm*

h. da*mn*
I. *nov*ice
j. *op*era
k. *st*ride
l. *tu*ndra
m. *xy*lophone

92. WORD WITH THE SUFFIX -OLOGY

1. geology	14. astrology
2. sociology	15. dermatology
3. neurology	16. zoology
4. cosmetology	17. technology
5. pathology	18. paleontology
6. theology	19. psychology
7. biology	20. archaeology
8. entomology	21. physiology
9. ecology	22. etmyology
10. musicology	23. anthropology
11. petrology	24. pharmacology
12. toxicology	25. kinesiology
13. meteorology	

The three names are: EINSTEIN, CURIE, and GALEN. They're associated with science.

The Land of Literature

Word Games 93–112

93. DO YOU HAVE THE MIDAS TOUCH?

1.	F		9.	B
2.	O		10.	E
3.	L		11.	I
4.	P		12.	K
5.	J		13.	D
6.	H		14.	A
7.	N		15.	C
8.	G		16.	M

94. AMERICAN WRITERS' WORD FIND

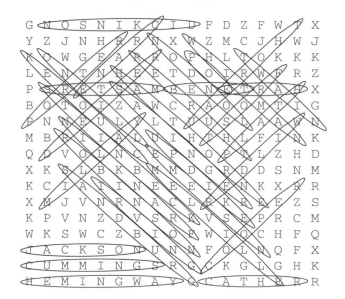

95. ONOMATO WHAT???

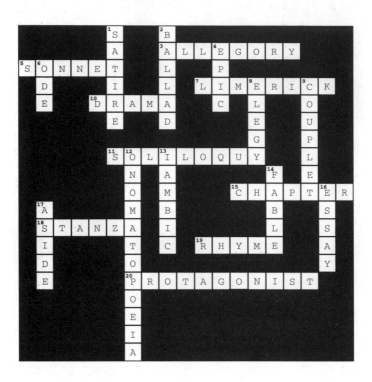

96. SWISH, BOOM, BAM!

Possible onomatopoeic words found in the grid are:

baa	konk
bang	moo
boo	ooze
bowwow	pow
buzz	wallop
clang	yank
coo	zap
boom	zip
bonk	zonk
hiss	zoom

97. DON'T READ THESE BOOKS!

98. OBJECTION! I WANT THAT BOOK BANNED RIGHT NOW!!

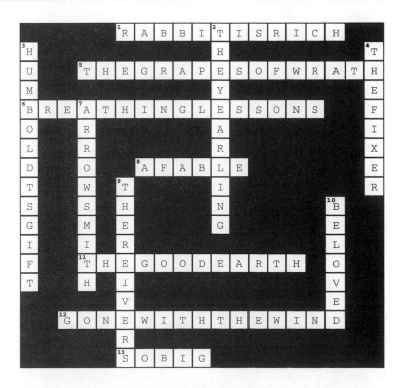

99. THE FOOD OF LITERATURE

1. E - Raisin
2. F (or T) - Grapes
3. K - Apple
4. L - Orange
5. J - Cherry
6. O - Chocolate
7. P - Pea
8. B - Fudge
9. H - Fish
10. R - Duck

11. Q - Cakes
12. S - Rabbit
13. F (or T) - Tortilla
14. N - Rabbit
15. M - Egg
16. I - Eggs, Ham
17. G - Rabbit
18. A - Deer
19. D - Goose
20. C - Rye

100. THE FORMS OF LITERATURE

1. epic
2. diary
3. speech
4. legend
5. essay
6. fairy tale
7. folk tale

8. journal
9. biography
10. autobiography
11. novel
12. play
13. poem
14. short story
15. thesis

101. THE TERMS OF THEATRICAL PRODUCTIONS

102. LITERARY RHYME TIME

1. Herman's Germans
2. Walt's salts
3. Cooper's snoopers
4. Earnest Ernest
5. Curt Kurt
6. Plath's wraths
7. Miller's tillers
8. Hughes' views
9. Yeats' mates
10. Pound's mounds
11. Lost Frost
12. Jane's pains
13. Homer's roamers
14. Toni's ponies
15. Lorraine's terrains
16. Pope's ropes
17. Blake's cakes
18. Keat's seats
19. Shelley's jellies
20. Joyce's choices

103. THE TOOLS OF POETRY

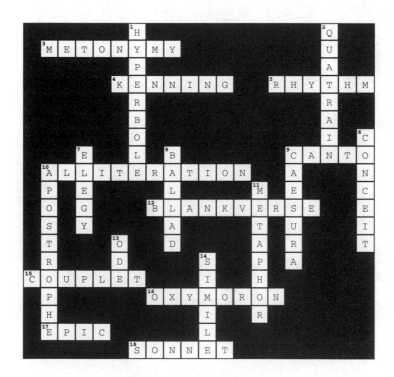

104. UNSCRAMBLING POETIC TERMS

1. ACCENT
2. ALLEGORY
3. ALLUSION
13. EUPHONY
14. FOOT
15. HAIKU

4. ANAPEST	16. IAMB
5. APOSTROPHE	17. IRONY
6. ASSONANCE	18. LIMERICK
7. BALLAD	19. METAPHOR
8. BLANK VERSE	20. METONYMY
9. CACOPHONY	21. PARADOX
10. CAESURA	22. QUATRAIN
11. COUPLET	23. RHYTHM
12. DACTYL	24. SCANSION

105. MORE POETIC TERMS

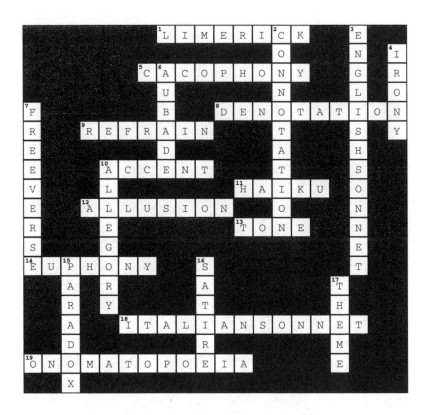

106. THE POETS' PLACE

1. Who shall set a limit to the influence of a human being?

Ralph Waldo Emerson

2. Education is the ability to listen to almost anything without losing your temper or your self-confidence.

Robert Frost

3. A poet is, before anything else, a person who is passionately in love with language.

W.H. Auden

Real letters: A B C D E F G H I J K L M N O P Q R S T U V W X Y Z
Substitute letters: R E Y Z I K M X D Q L F T A U S H V N G W O P C J B

107. POPULAR MAGAZINES

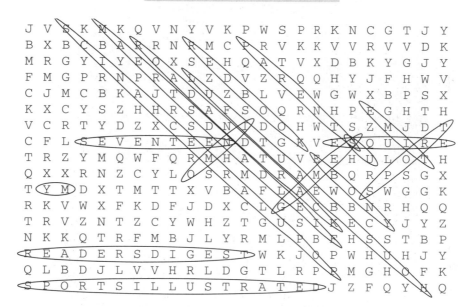

108. LITERARY TITLES IN FRENCH

1. n	11. s
2. f	12. q
3. g	13. b
4. e	14. r
5. m	15. t
6. o	16. k
7. h	17. j
8. c	18. i
9. a	19. d
10. l	20. p

109. BIBLICALLY SPEAKING

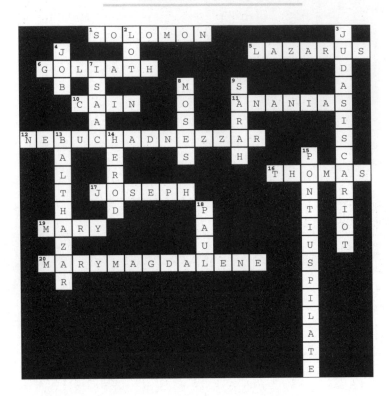

110. QUOTABLE QUOTES

1. (d)   No man is an island.
2. (j)   I have a dream.
3. (f)   Good fences make good neighbors.
4. (h)   A thing of beauty is a joy forever.
5. (b)   O my Luve's like a red, red rose.
6. (e)   A penny saved is a penny earned.
7. (g)   Gather ye rosebuds while ye may.
8. (c)   It was the best of times, it was the worst of times.
9. (a)   How do I love thee? Let me count the ways.
10. (i)   Poems are made by fools like me, but only God can make a tree.

111. ROYALTY IN LITERARY TITLES

1. Count
2. Prince
3. Queen
4. Lord

11. King
12. Emperor
13. Rex (King)
14. Princess

5.	King	15. Emperor
6.	Princess	16. Princess
7.	King	17. Duchess
8.	King	18. Lord
9.	Lord	19. King
10.	Prince	20. Duke

112. SHAKESPEARE'S FAMOUS THIRTEEN

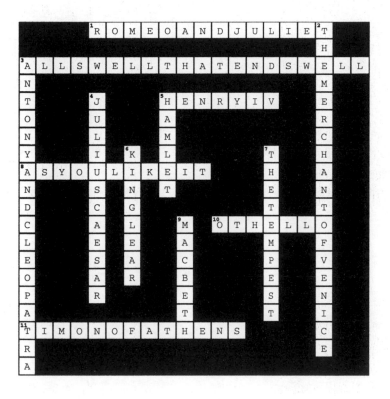

Making Language Work for You

Word Games 113–141

113. BET ON A TIE

1.	S	8.	RO
2.	F	9.	F
3.	F	10.	S
4.	RO	11.	F
5.	S	12.	S
6.	RO	13.	S
7.	S		

Each contestant gained *nine* lengths.

114. AN EVEN DOZEN

SET 1			SET 2		
A.	RO	3	A.	F	2
B.	S	1	B.	RO	3
C.	F	2	C.	S	1
D.	S	1	D.	F	2
E.	F	2	E.	F	2
F.	RO	3	F.	F	2

115. DIRECT ME TO YOUR OBJECT!

1.	guard	6.	rim
2.	shot	7.	stuff
3.	substitute	8.	travel
4.	uniforms	9.	swish
5.	baskets	10.	net

The direct objects are all associated with *basketball*.

116. THE PLANE FLEW _____ THE CLOUDS

1. to Harry's old mother
2. After Sunday
3. near Arlington
4. Near Connie's yacht
5. during intermission
6. against nine Eskimos
7. by Rita's interesting American niece.
8. On Sunday, concerning Ayn Rand
9. by Eddie, to Tom Young
10. for lunch
11. On any routine Thursday

The four boys' names are Thomas, Brian, Oscar, and Art.
The four girls' names are Nancy, Diane, Betty, and Flo.

117. A SCORE OF ADVERBS FOR THE TAKING

1. crudely
2. yesterday, readily
3. usually, silently
4. meekly, casually
5. cautiously
6. openly, rashly
7. merely, inanely, cowardly
8. keenly
9. rarely, exactly
10. apparently, precisely
11. evenly
12. rigidly

The inventor is *Cyrus McCormick* and his invention is the *reaper*.

118. WEARING DIFFERENT HATS

1. adjective
2. verb
3. noun
4. preposition
5. conjunction
6. preposition
7. verb
8. adverb
9. adjective
10. noun
11. verb
12. adjective
13. noun
14. noun
15. verb

Oh, I can barely go to the game since I have little money.
int. pro. v.   adv.   v. prp. adj.   n.   conj. pro. v.   adj.   n.

119. TWO BY TWO BY TWO BY TWO BY TWO . . .

1. left	6.	nobody
2. Aviation	7.	ugly
3. ewe	8.	Ha
4. elegantly	9.	lower
5. Leo	10.	Neither

Leave well enough alone.

120. GRANDMA KNOWS GRAMMAR!

1. L	9.	A
2. K	10.	E
3. I	11.	D
4. O	12.	J
5. C	13.	M
6. H	14.	P
7. N	15.	B
8. F	16.	G

Bonus: Grandma Moses gained fame in the field of painting.

121. THE VERB'S THE WORD

1. watered	7.	intimidate
2. has	8.	shuffled
3. enlisted	9.	added
4. needs	10.	justified
5. inched	11.	answered
6. terrified	12.	replied

When is a door not a door? When it is ajar!

122. HOW IRREGULAR!

1. driven	7. brought
2. done	8. come
3. taken	9. began
4. ate	10. given
5. fell	11. saw
6. ridden	12. went

The famous American personality is RONALD REAGAN.

123. "THE BRITISH ARE COMING! THE BRITISH ARE COMING!"

1. price	9. racquetball
2. anybody	10. enjoyment
3. Ulysses	11. bouquet
4. Larry	12. Ornithology
5. research	13. study
6. Existentialism	14. terminology
7. Vincent	15. ostriches
8. everything	16. none

The famous Ameican is PAUL REVERE and the city is BOSTON.

124. "I DONE GOOD!"

1. have	8. beside
2. teach	9. anywhere
3. less	10. somewhat
4. I	11. whom
5. well	12. any
6. between	13. way
7. effect	14. is
	15. let

125. IS IT HE AND I OR HE AND ME?

GROUP ONE

Answer/Points

A. He and I (1)
B. they (1)
C. whom (4)
D. they (3)
E. me (3)
F. she (4)

GROUP TWO

Answer/Points

A. her and me (6)
B. Bob and her (4)
C. My sister and they (2)
D. I (2)
E. I (2)

Each group has a total of 16.

126. "DON'T SAY, 'EACH GIRL HAS THEIR PURSE.'"

1. performs
2. are
3. kicks
4. increase
5. Several
6. touches
7. are
8. neither
9. teach
10. understands
11. respond
12. kids
13. expands
14. yell

The two countries are *Pakistan* and *Turkey*.

127. CAPITAL LETTERS

The words that are capitalized are:

1. Nicole, Oliver, Tallahassee, Europe.
2. All, Red, Sox, Indianapolis, Norman, Thomas, Hudson.
3. Edna, Wellings, Rhode, Island, Texas.
4. Everybody, Reds.
5. Neither, Ophelia's.

6.   Thomas, Edison, American, Rod, Serling.
7.   Isaac, Newton's.
8.   To, Harvard, Edgar, Rice.
9.   Eventually, Anno, Domini.
10. Educational, Research, Foundation, Roberta, Olsen, Super, Tuesday.

   Quote: No tears in the writer, no tears in the reader. (Frost)

128. DON'T DON'T REPEAT REPEAT YOURSELF YOURSELF

Listed below are the unnecessary or repetitive words.

1.   right here or on this spot
2.   young
3.   small or petite
4.   above his eyes
5.   to our eyes
6.   he
7.   of four people
8.   single
9.   at any time
10. and always
11. that hold liquids
12. who writes
13. self-operating
14. alone or by herself
15. also or too

129. THE PRONUNCIATION OF WORDS

1.   L   fuel
2.   C   parquet
3.   I   queue
4.   H   phalanx
5.   D   aegis
6.   A   guise
7.   E   hiatus
8.   G   elegy
9.   F   xenophobia
10. J   wry
11. B   scald
12. K   tumult

130. A LETTER FROM CAMP

Line number   Corrections

1.   It's, since, I , you, There
2.   write, our, weather
3.   week, I'll, by
4.   we, here, There, horses, hares, bears, does

5. night, two, rowed, past, their
6. for, hours
7. counselor, to, shore, One
8. principal, waving
9. plane, Then, life, loose
10. male, counselor, altogether
11. some, advice, What, he
12. not, complimentary, peaceful, scene, moral
13. tale, waste, time, know, who's
14. write
15. Sincerely
16. your, son

131. WHICH WORD IS RIGHT?

1.	scene	9.	vain
2.	quite	10.	know
3.	its	11.	have
4.	passed	12.	stationary
5.	morale	13.	loose
6.	sole	14.	set
7.	threw	15.	canvass
8.	whether		

The two words often confused are *ascent* and *assent*.

132. WHEN TO CITE THE SITE AND ALLUDE TO THE ILLUSION

A.	pour	H.	meat
B.	quite	I.	feigned
C.	amount	J.	right
D.	cent	K.	seem
E.	allusion	L.	pain
F.	flair	M.	vane
G.	well	N.	there

The two South American countries are *Argentina* and *Chile*.

133. THOSE CONFUSING WORDS!

1. affect
2. all ready
3. berth
4. number
5. flair
6. less
7. council
8. mettle

9. seam
10. heel
11. waist
12. your
13. personnel
14. principal
15. pane

The three confusing words are: *cent, scent,* and *sent.*

134. IS THIS DONE FORMALLY OR FORMERLY?

1. A
2. K
3. S
4. H
5. B
6. J
7. C
8. O
9. T
10. D

11. Q
12. G
13. E
14. L
15. F
16. P
17. I
18. R
19. N
20. M

135. IS A BICYCLE STATIONARY OR STATIONERY?

1. O
2. N
3. P
4. K
5. M
6. H
7. E
8. Q
9. F
10. C

11. D
12. J
13. A
14. R
15. I
16. B
17. S
18. G
19. T
20. L

136. HOMOPHONES

1. quartz

2. onyx

3. child

4. mews

Bonus: Homophones and their definitions for the words above are:

1. need: require, Lou: a man's name, holy: sacred, main: most important (or Maine: a state), hanger: used for hanging things, fourth: following the third

2. hew: carve, hail: ice or salute, feet: plural of foot, feint: a fake attack

3. colonel: military rank, chorale: chorus, core: central part, canvas: cloth, course: path or class

4. doe: female deer, bell: something you ring, earn: work for, burro: an animal (or burrow: to dig)

137. HOMONYMS—KNOWING WHEN TO USE WHAT

1.	wailing	11.	while
2.	their	12.	knows
3.	stare	13.	rood
4.	isle	14.	deer
5.	stake	15.	mane
6.	read	16.	knew
7.	dough	17.	rest
8.	reel	18.	seize
9.	site	19.	bore
10.	whether	20.	stile

138. HAVEN'T I HEARD THAT BEFORE?

1.	f	sea	13.	t	hale
2.	x	thrown	14.	c	mite
3.	k	lone	15.	j	knight
4.	y	groan	16.	p	weigh
5.	q	wheel	17.	w	muscle
6.	a	wile	18.	b	vain
7.	v	seas	19.	i	vale

8.	e	aisle	20.	o	steal
9.	l	weight	21.	d	shoo
10.	g	through	22.	m	deer
11.	n	pear	23.	s	bow
12.	h	shear	24.	r	grate
			25.	u	scene

139. FIND THE OTHER WORD

1. **ballet**: a type of dance
2. **ballot**: a method of voting
3. **collage**: a type of art
4. **college**: place of learning after high school
5. **pole**: a long stick
6. **poll**: vote
7. **precede**: to come before
8. **proceed**: to move forward
9. **rain**: precipitation
10. **reign**: royal power
11. **rein**: narrow strip of leather
12. **ring**: to sound
13. **statue**: a piece of sculpture
14. **statute**: a law
15. **tenant**: an occupant
16. **tenet**: a rule
17. **tortuous**: twisting
18. **torturous**: involving pain
19. **way**: a route
20. **whey**: thick, watery part of milk
21. **wring**: to twist

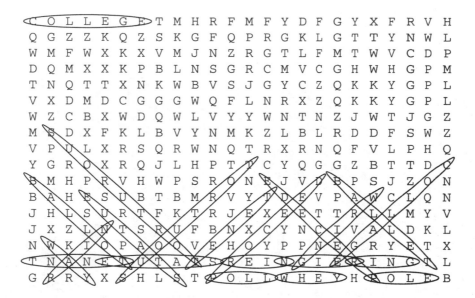

140. A CONFUSING CROSSWORD PUZZLE

141. ARE YOU ADEPT ENOUGH TO ADAPT?

Taking the Tests by the Horns

Word Games 142–163

142. A BEVY OF B'S

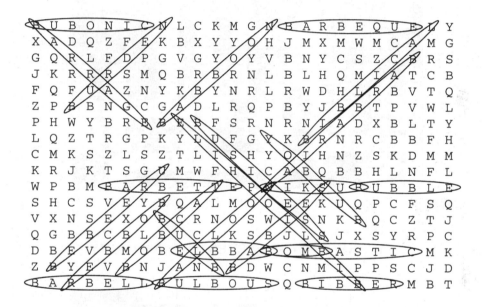

143. FROM A TO Z

144. ARE YOU INDIFFERENT TO ANARCHY?

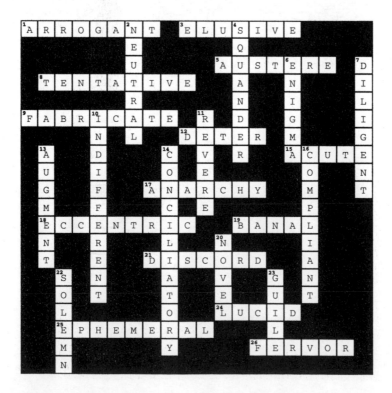

145. RACKING UP ON THE S.A.T.

INCREMENT · LITIGATE · PARSIMONIOUS · ADVERSE · PRUDENT · CRYPTIC · BRAWN · SKEPTICAL · MONOLITHIC · TACITURN · PENCHANT · PAUCITY · EXTRICATE

STRINGENT · PRELIARATE · MERGER · FIDDLING · SORROGG · PROGNOG · CACOPHONY · ILLICIT · VINDICTIVE · PROFUSE

146. THE E–Z PUZZLE

EXHAUSTIVE · EXE · EQUITABLE · ELICIT · EXHORT · ENDEMIC · ZOOLOGY · ZODIAC · EMINENT · ZEPHYR · ZANY · ECCENTRIC

ESOTERIC · ENIGMA · ERUDITE · ENERGREG · EGREGIOUS · ZIGZAG · ZITHER · ZEAL · EDIFY

147. FIT TO A "T"

148. SUCCESS ON THE STANDARDIZED TESTS

149. S.A.T. WORD UNSCRAMBLING

1.	abolish	21.	vanish
2.	descend	22.	wharf
3.	endure	23.	parole
4.	jeopardy	24.	negate
5.	tyrant	25.	debtor
6.	obese	26.	cleave
7.	discard	27.	shrill
8.	soothe	28.	idol
9.	vague	29.	rue
10.	wry	30.	quirk
11.	jaded	31.	archaic
12.	biped	32.	edify
13.	dross	33.	elegy
14.	dole	34.	effigy
15.	urbane	35.	thesis
16.	stigma	36.	alibi
17.	concur	37.	pique
18.	schism	38.	lucid
19.	tyro	39.	trauma
20.	purse	40.	tithe

150. MANY WAYS TO SAY HAPPY

1.	pleased	9.	contented
2.	gay	10.	tickled
3.	satisfied	11.	cheerful
4.	delighted	12.	elated
5.	merry	13.	jovial
6.	jolly	14.	blithe
7.	thrilled	15.	jocund
8.	joyful		

Real letters: A B C D E F G H I J K L M N O P Q R S T U V W X Y Z
Substitute letters: G M U L P C F V N K A O E Q J W R B X Z H D T S I Y

151. A SHELTER'S SAFETY

1.   haven
2.   refuge
3.   asylum
4.   harbor
5.   hideout
6.   safety
7.   cave
8.   recess
9.   nook
10. den
11. niche
12. mew
13. dugout
14. fortress
15. safehold

One of America's most famous shelters is *FORT TICONDEROGA*.

152. PARADISE IN OTHER WORDS

The other words found in the word grid are: Eden, Elysium, Heaven, Jubile, Olympus, Utopia, Xanadu, and Zion.

153. FRIEND OR FOE OR NO CONNECTION?

1.   S
2.   A
3.   A
4.   NC
5.   A
6.   A
7.   A
8.   NC
9.   A
10. S
11. A
12. A
13. S
14. NC
15. NC
16. A
17. A
18. S
19. S
20. NC
21. A
22. A
23. S
24. NC
25. A
26. S
27. NC
28. A
29. A
30. NC
31. A
32. S
33. NC
34. A
35. NC
36. NC

154. GREAT HANGMAN WORDS

1.   tryst
2.   queue
3.   nth
4.   rhythm
5.   quixotic
13. dyad
14. kayak
15. byte
16. mnemonic
17. hype

6. myrrh
7. phylum
8. usury
9. zinc
10. phlegm
11. whey
12. gym

18. unctuous
19. vex
20. faze
21. gypsum
22. gyro
23. whelp
24. eke
25. lymph

155. PHOBOPHOBIA

1. g
2. c
3. j
4. m
5. o
6. i
7. e

8. b
9. d
10. l
11. n
12. k
13. h
14. f
15. a

156. SAME OR OPPOSITE?

1. S
2. A
3. A
4. A
5. S
6. A
7. S
8. S
9. A
10. A

11. S
12. A
13. S
14. A
15. S
16. S
17. A
18. S
19. S
20. S

The hidden author is Emily Bronte.

157. S.A.T. ANALOGY QUESTIONS

Though some questions may have more than one answer, possible answers include:

1. C	5. D	9. C	13. G
2. D	6. E	10. C	14. E
3. C	7. E	11. G	15. C
4. D	8. A	12. F	16. B

158. S.A.T. ANALOGIES MATCHUP

1. G.	7. D
2. A	8. E
3. I	9. B
4. L	10. F
5. C	11. K
6. H	12. J

The two girls' names are *Gail* (#1–4) and *Deb* (#7–9).

159. S.A.T. COMPLETIONS...THE DEFINITIONS

1. deceive, mislead, delude
2. benefactress, philanthropist
3. redundant, repetitive
4. hasty, rash, careless
5. exacting, rigorous, painstaking
6. boring, soporific, tedious
7. covert, clandestine, surreptitious
8. enigmatic, inexplicable, abstruse
9. apathetic, indifferent, incurious
10. misdemeanor, peccadillo

160. S.A.T. SENTENCE COMPLETIONS...COMPLETING THE IDEA

Possible answers include:

1.	well, beautifully, outstandingly	6.	averse, reluctant
2.	outstanding, excellent, splendid	7.	unpredictable, erratic
3.	hard, assiduously, ambitiously	8.	agreeable, temperate

4. loud, deafening, grating   9. scared, frightened

5. volatile, tense   10. anxious, eager

161. S.A.T. SENTENCE COMPLETIONS...REVERSING THE IDEA

Possible answers include:

1. honest, credible, trustworthy
2. well, impressively
3. poor, low, unacceptable
4. bad, unsatisfactory
5. maverick, nonconformist, individualist
6. boring...stimulating; interesting...tedious
7. terrific...horrendous; inferior...quality
8. Impassive...emotional; humorous...serious
9. dangerous...smoke; harmful...crave
10. months, years

162. UNSCRAMBLED MEATS BECOME STEAM!

1. shore   11. swap
2. stone   12. signer
3. lisp   13. letters
4. wrest   14. carter
5. range   15. wrong
6. angel   16. angle
7. below   17. readded
8. regal   18. baser
9. steak   19. sham
10. steal   20. sweat

163. WHEN A WORD BECOMES A WARD

1. compose, compost   10. haven, maven
2. truckle, trickle   11. feast, yeast
3. lease,leash   12. yodel, model
4. numb, dumb   13. feign,reign
5. steak, speak   14. gnarl, snarl

6. marry, tarry
7. plump, plumb
8. dusk, musk
9. grove, grave

15. towel, vowel
16. cutter, gutter
17. pester, fester
18. tallow, wallow

Bonus: The boy's name is Gary Swift.

Just Plain Fun

Word Games 164–201

164. AND THE CATEGORY IS

	Animals	Authors	Sports	U.S. Cities	Girls' Names
S	skunk	Shakespeare	swimming	Sacramento, California	Susan
T	tiger	Twain	track	Tampa, Florida	Thelma
A	aardvark	Alcott	auto racing	Augusta, Maine (Georgia)	Andrea
R	rabbit	Roth	roller derby	Richmond, Virginia	Regina
E	elephant	Ellison	free	Eugene, Oregon	Ellen

These are possible answers.

165. BIG AND SMALL

Possible answers including the word *big* or *small* include:

BIG

Big Apple (NYC)

big band (type of music)

Big bang theory (cosmology theory)

Big Board (New York Stock Exchange listings)

Big Brother (*1984* character)

big game (large wild animals hunted for sport)

big house (slang for penitentiary)

big intestine (body part)

big league (highest level)

big mouth (person who talks too much)

Big River (Broadway play)

big shot (a person of importance)

big stick (political position backed by strength)

Big Ten (NCAA athletic conference)

Big East (NCAA athletic conference)

big time (highest professional level)

big top (circus)

Little Big Horn (Custer's Last Stand)

Little Big Man (movie)

Big Top (circus)

SMALL

small arms (firearms of small caliber)

small change (something that has little value)

small forward (a basketball position)

small fry (a person who is small, young, or short)

small game (small hunted animals)

small hours (the time after midnight)

small intestine (a body part)

small-minded (prejudiced)

smallmouth bass (a fish)

small potatoes (an insignificant person or event)

small scale (on a reduced level)

small screen (television)

small-town (unsophisticated)

166. BUILDING BLOCKS CONTEST

Answers will vary.

167. CAN YOU MAKE A WILLOW WALLOW?

1. believe, relieve
2. crown, drown
3. sleet, sheet
4. white, while
5. master, muster
6. grove, trove
7. cover, hover
8. pest, zest
9. fright, bright

10. suffer, buffer
11. ghastly, ghostly
12. ream, read
13. destitution, restitution
14. hollow, hallow
15. fellow, mellow
16. clove, close

Bonus: fold, gold, hold

168. CATCHING SOME Z'S

1. muzzle
2. puzzle
3. frazzle
4. nozzle
5. fizzle
6. drizzle
7. embezzle

8. sizzle
9. bedazzle
10. frizzle
11. guzzle
12. razzle
13. dazzle

All words end with the *le* combination.

169. COMBINING WORDS

1. starting
2. establish
3. flaunted
4. resorted or restored
5. global
6. pander
7. sheared
8. latent or talent

9. bridled
10. fragrance
11. throwing
12. warmest
13. dative
14. probate
15. earnestly

170. A COMMON LETTER

1. U. . .rout, feud, louse
2. V. . .liven, shove, rove
3. R. . .broom, drove, cart
4. F. . .flame, defer, flag
5. W. . .swank, twang, swore
6. Y. . .yeast, dyad, decoy
7. N. . .divan, dozen, spend
8. L. . .clone, realm, dolt
9. C. . .cable, recap, mince
10. E. . .glade, stare, rube
11. D. . .sander, hide, grind
12. T. . .wart, spurt, tease
13. E. . .tear, peat, least
14. B. . .blame, gable, broom

171. CUTTING DOWN WORDS

1. DRAIN   RAIN   RAN   AN   A
2. SHORT   SORT   ORT   OR   O
3. GRAND   GRAN   RAN   AN   A
4. AMORALLY   MORALLY   ORALLY   RALLY   ALLY   ALL   AL   A
5. BLEND   LEND   LED   ED
6. FEAST   FEAT   EAT   AT   A
7. SPRITE   SPITE   SPIT   PIT   PI   I
8. CHASTE   HASTE   HATE   HAT   AT   A
9. STILLED   TILLED   TILED   TILE   TIE   TI   I
10. WANDER   WADER   WADE   ADE   AD   A
11. SHRED   SHED   SHE   HE
12. SPRINT   PRINT   PINT   PIN   IN   I
13. TRAIL   TAIL   AIL   AL   A
14. GLOBE   LOBE   LOB   LO   O

172. FUN WITH WORDS

1. racecar
2. gaga (aga)
3. settle (Seattle)
4. gherkin (her kin)
5. caper (cpr)
6. grapple (gape)
7. scatter (shatter, smatter, spatter, swatter)
8. mundane (Dane)
9. emulate (lame Ute)
10. leper (repel)

173. HIDDEN WORDS

1. i-finish
2. f-foreign
3. b-stamen
4. m-offend
5. e-lapse
6. l-start
7. a-callow
8. k-invent
9. n-trickle
10. j-assess
11. o-notice
12. c-yearn
13. h-unity
14. d-swear
15. g-stipend

174. THE INITIALS' GAME

Answers will vary.

175. JUST HORSIN' AROUND

1. to<u>ke</u>n
2. men<u>ti</u>on
3. st<u>uc</u>k
4. trick<u>y</u>
5. pru<u>de</u>nt
6. bar<u>be</u>d
7. <u>cy</u>press
8. ar<u>re</u>st
9. ste<u>ak</u>
10. un<u>e</u>ven
11. fruitle<u>ss</u>
12. pro<u>be</u>
13. rea<u>lm</u>
14. bat<u>on</u>
15. en<u>tr</u>ap
16. <u>ac</u>cessory
17. <u>e</u>stablish

The *Kentucky Derby, Preakness,* (and) *Belmont races* are famous horse races.

176. THE LETTER LINEUP

1. astro
2. cat
3. liar
9. armor
10. port
11. rail

4. tuba
5. he
6. Ophelia
7. sat
8. but

12. kilt
13. bad
14. abut
15. ail
16. tack
17. tub
18. catastrophe

177. LOOKING FOR SOME FUN?

1. funnel
2. refund
3. fundamental
4. affluence
5. function
6. funeral
7. funky
8. foundation
9. found
10. defunct

11. furnace
12. furniture
13. fraudulent
14. fountain
15. flounder
16. fund
17. fecund
18. funny
19. fungus
20. influence

178. THE MONTHS OF THE YEAR

1. janitor
2. myopia
3. augur
4. junior
5. novice
6. octagon
7. septet
8. capricious
9. jewel
10. julep

11. febrile
12. martinet
13. decide
14. nightmare
15. bigamy
16. innovate
17. inaugurate
18. doctor
19. decade
20. jangle

The man after whom the seventh month is named is JULIUS CAESAR.

179. MOVE ALONG, LITTLE LETTER!

1. ten
2. stun
3. attend
4. mistreat
5. chaotic
6. majesty
7. adamant

8. systematic
9. magistrate
10. resentment
11. commandment
12. retrenchment
13. graniloquent

Bonus: tatty

180. OLD AGE IS IN!

Possible answers for words having the word *old* in them are:
behold, beholden, bold, cold, doldrums, embolden, fold, gold, golden, mold, olden, refold, resold, retold, scold, sold, solder, soldier, told.

Possible answers for words having the word *age* in them are:
aged, agency, agenda, agent, cage, decoupage, dotage, flagella, homage, image, lager, manage, menagerie, page, pageant, rage, sage, sager, stage, wage, wager.

181. NO P'S PLEASE!

1. pepper or peer
2. passport
3. paper
4. preppie
5. paprika
6. papyrus
7. papaya
8. flapper
9. appendage
10. beeper
11. copper
12. upper
13. caper

14. wiper
15. epoxy
16. crepe
17. replica
18. propeller
19. opposition
20. foppish
21. zipper
22. pepsin
23. lymph
24. happy
25. express

Note: Other words may fit as answers.

182. A PAGE OF SINS

Possible answers with the word *sin* in them are:
basin, business, casino, cosine, disintegrate, moccasin, pepsin, resin, sine, sinecure, sinew, sinful, sing, singe, single, singlet, singular, sinister, sink.

183. SDRAWKCAB SDROW

1. door-rood
2. star-rats
3. mart-tram
4. deer-reed
5. part-trap
6. remit-timer
7. room-moor
8. devil-lived
9. stab-bats
10. stew-wets
11. namer-reman
12. regas-sager
13. pots-stop
14. drawer-reward
15. lever-revel
16. straw-warts

Bonus: state-etats

184. A NUMBER OF THINGS

1. 76 trombones led the Big Parade
2. 60 minutes in an hour
3. 4 seasons in a year
4. 2001 Space Odyssey
5. 57 Heinz varieties
6. 12 Days of Christmas
7. 7 days in a week
8. 13 original colonies
9. 12 inches in a foot

10. 1760 yards in a mile
11. 24 hours in a day
12. 12 tribes of Israel
13. 100 years in a century
14. 1000 years in a millenium
15. 3.14 equals pi
16. 14 lines in a sonnet
17. 2 nickels in a dime
18. 14 days in a fortnight
19. 10 years in a decade
20. 20 years in a score

185. THERE'S A LIE IN EVERY ONE OF THESE!

1.	F	12.	P
2.	K	13.	T
3.	L	14.	D
4.	Q	15.	I
5.	B	16.	S
6.	E	17.	J
7.	R	18.	H
8.	V	19.	O
9.	M	20.	U
10.	G	21.	C
11.	A	22.	N

186. WORDS FROM WELL KNOWN PEOPLE

1. He was not of an age, but for all time! Ben Jonson (said of William Shakespeare)
2. I am not young enough to know everything. J.M. Barrie (author of *Peter Pan*)
3. Let us never negotiate out of fear, but let us never fear to negotiate. John F. Kennedy

Real letters: A B C D E F G H I J K L M N O P Q R S T U V W X Y Z

Substitute letters: I N G Y M Z B U D F J W A R C L S V Q E X T O H P K

187. X MARKS THE SPOT

1. flux
2. wax
3. ax
4. pax
5. vortex
6. sox
7. helix
8. suffix

9. vex
10. prefix
11. hex
12. apex
13. flex
14. redux
15. lynx

Bonus Answer: private eye

188. THE EAR EXAM

1. yellow fellow
2. mild child
3. no doe
4. late Nate
5. church birch
6. large barge
7. wrong song
8. bleaker sneaker
9. new stew
10. stage rage

11. red Ted
12. rude dude
13. silly billy
14. muddy buddy
15. colder boulder
16. Tallahassee lassie
17. obese geese
18. great fate
19. ten yen
20. Betty's Getty's

189. RHYMIN' SIMON

1. big rig
2. Nixon's vixens
3. George's gorges
4. hare's cares
5. funny bunny
6. Willie's billies
7. Leno's stenos
8. Clark's narcs
9. Paul's malls
10. Billy's fillies

11. Joan's bones
12. Carter's barters
13. Curie's furies
14. Michael's cycles (or Mike's bikes)
15. Groucho's gauchos
16. Mark's barks
17. Rather's lathers
18. Bill's bills
19. Al's pals
20. Yale's tales

190. GEORGE WASHINGTON

1. Revolutionary
2. Planter
3. Virginia
4. Mount Vernon
5. Martha
6. Continental Congress
7. Commander-in-Chief
8. Yorktown
9. Inauguration
10. Weems
11. Stuart
12. Adams
13. Pneumonia
14. Indian
15. Wood

Bonus Answer: cherry tree

191. OUR SIXTEENTH PRESIDENT

1. label
2. saber
3. absolute
4. cabaret
5. jabber
6. enable
7. fabricate
8. abet
9. disable
10. caliber
11. abbreviate
12. marble
13. babble
14. drabness
15. established
16. strawberry

The term associated with Abe Lincoln is CIVIL WAR.

192. THE PRESIDENT'S RESIDENCE

1. Polk's folks
2. Hoover's louvers
3. Chester's jesters
4. Teddy's eddies
5. Flaxen Jackson
6. Monroe's foes
7. Grant's ants
8. Tyler's stylers
9. Cal's pals
10. Bush's bushes
11. Bill's bills
12. Roosevelt's pelts
13. George's forges
14. Harrison's garrisons
15. Reagan's pagans
16. Ford's boards
17. Carter's carters
18. Hayes' daze
19. Taylor's whalers

193. WORDS HAVING MEN'S NAMES IN THEM

1. adamant
2. benevolent
3. jacket
4. billiards
5. stevedore
6. philology
7. fluke
8. willful
9. eddy
10. martinet

11. corduroy
12. salvation
13. elbow
14. shank
15. cordon
16. gleeful
17. séance
18. frankincense
19. kenning
20. frond

194. HIDDEN GIRLS' NAMES

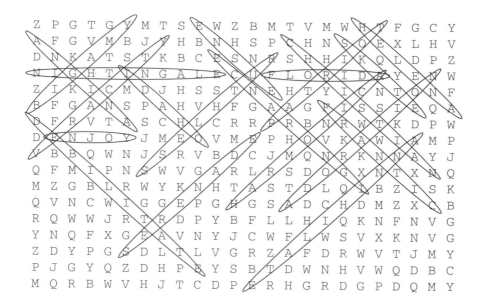

bigamy	frantic	enjoy	patriot
annihilate	nightingale	skate	ruthless
Christian	angina	Florida	serenade
debilitate	Helena	harmonica	ensue
adoration	Idaho	ignorance	veracity

195. GIRLS' NAMES IN OTHER WORDS

1.	H	11.	T
2.	Q	12.	D
3.	L	13.	K
4.	M	14.	I
5.	O	15.	P
6.	A	16.	F
7.	J	17.	N
8.	E	18.	R
9.	B	19.	S
10.	C	20.	G

196. GET A JOB!

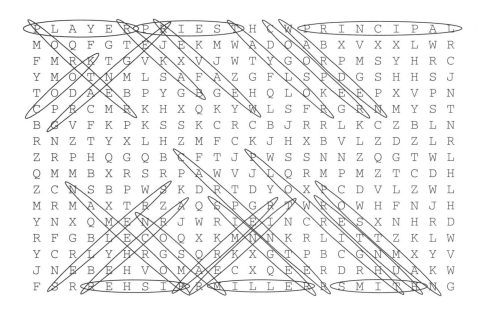

Anne Archer - actress

Carrie Fisher - actress

Dennis Weaver - actor

Fanny Farmer - cooking writer

James Cook - explorer

James Mason - actor

James Taylor - singer

James Fenimore Cooper - author

Gary Player - golfer   Joan Plowright - actress
George Foreman- boxer   Judas Priest - musical talent
Gov. Al Smith - politician   Karen Carpenter - singer
Grant Tinker - producer   Katherine Anne Porter - author
Holly Hunter - actress   Neil Postman - author and educator
Isaac Bashevis Singer - author   Peter Sellers - actor
Jack Warden - actor   Steve Miller - singer/musician
James Baker - politician   Stuart Granger - actor
                                        Victoria Principal - actress

197. GEOFFREY WHO?

1. Shakespeare (shake + spear)
2. Mansfield (man's + field)
3. Updike (up + dike)
4. Milton (mill + ton)
5. Dickinson (dick + in + son)
6. Plato (play + toe)
7. Hemingway (hemming + way)
8. Sterne (stern)
9. Wordsworth (word's + worth)
10. Welty (welt + e)
11. Alcott (al + cot)
12. Wilde (wild)

198. HAVE A WHALE OF A TIME WITH THESE MEN

1. menthol
2. management
3. rudimentary
4. commend
5. lament
6. mendicant
7. merriment
8. cement
9. menial
10. environment
11. ointment
12. Mendel
13. momentarily
14. basement

The hidden name is HERMAN MELVILLE, the creator of Moby Dick, the famous white *whale.*

199. "DON'T BE SO CURT, CURT!"

1.	art	11.	frank
2.	bill	12.	hector
3.	bob	13.	jack
4.	carol	14.	lance
5.	chuck	15.	laurel
6.	don	16.	mark
7.	dot	17.	norm
8.	duke or earl	18.	ray
9.	eddy	19.	sue
10.	faith	20.	victor

200. COMMON LAST NAMES

1. Bradley — Bill: U. S. Senator... Ben: newspaper editor... Omar: U.S. General

2. Wright — Wilbur: inventor... Orville: inventor... Richard: author

3. Clinton — Bill: U.S. President... Hillary: First Lady... DeWitt: former governor of New York

4. Washington — George: first U.S. President... Booker T: U.S. educator and author... Martha: first First Lady

5. Marx — Karl: German Philosopher... Groucho: American entertainer... Harpo: American entertainer

6. Bronte — All three sisters were English authors

7. Lewis — Sinclair: American author... Jerry: American comedian and entertainer... C.S.: British writer

8. Lee — Robert E.: U.S. Confederate Army general... Pinky: American entertainer... Harper: American author

9. Irving — Clifford: American author... Washington: American author... John: American author

10. Thomas — Dylan: Welsh poet... Debi: American figure skater... Lowell: American traveler

11. Roosevelt — Teddy: U.S. President... Franklin: U.S.President... Eleanor: former First Lady

12. Taylor — Zachary: U.S. President... James: American singer... Lawrence: professional football player

13. Jones   Casey: train engineer... Bobby: former professional golfer... Quincy: American singer and songwriter

14. O'Connor   Sandra Day: Supreme Court Justice... Edwin: American author... Carroll: American actor

15. Williams   Tennessee: American playwright... Ted: Hall of Fame baseball player... William Carlos: American poet

16. Webster   Noah: American lexicographer... Daniel: U.S. orator... John: English dramatist

17. Wilson   August and Landford are both American playwrights... Willie: professional baseball player

18. Alou   All are former professional baseball players.

19. Madison   James: U.S. President... Dolly: First Lady... Oscar: character in *The Odd Couple*

20. John   Elton: British songwriter and singer... Olivia Newton: singer... Tommy: former professional baseball player

201. SPORTS CELEBRITIES

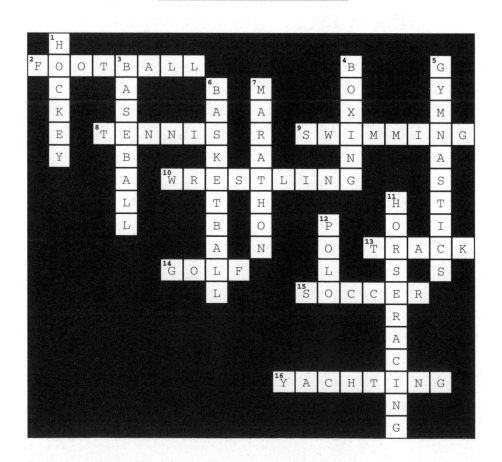

9